BOOKS

A Bite-Sized **Lifestyle** Book

Still Crazy About George Eliot 200 Years Later

A Joyful Celebration of Her Novels and Writing

22nd November 1819 – 22nd November 2019

edited by

Paul Davies

Cover by

Dean Stockton

Published by Bite-Sized Books Ltd 2019

Bite-Sized Books Ltd Cleeve Road, Goring RG8 9BJ UK
information@bite-sizedbooks.com
Registered in the UK.
Company Registration No: 9395379

ISBN: 9781702090872

Acknowledgements

Any book like this one which is a collaboration by over twenty writers benefits immensely from the input, suggestions, help and advice from each – and as editor I want to express my great appreciation for everyone who has contributed to making this volume worthy of George Eliot's birthday.

The Editor

Paul Davies has been a lifelong enthusiast for George Eliot's novels and completed his PhD, *George Eliot: Interpretations of a Society* in 1978. His main focus was on *Daniel Deronda*, which in the 1970s was regarded at best as idiosyncratic.

After teaching he joined the IT industry and had a long career in corporate life, lately as managing director of a US IT multinational in India, and then set up a management consultancy and a publishing company, Bite-Sized Books.

He conceived the idea of a celebratory book for George Eliot's 200th birthday for the 22nd November 2019 – she was born on 22nd November 1819 – and was joined by an enthusiastic group of writers and academics who have all written articles in a conversational, non-academic style with the express aim of encouraging people to read her wonderful novels.

Contents

Part 1: Her Remarkable Modern Life

How Mary Anne Evans (the future George Eliot) still shocks and surprises

Part 2: Her Surprising Heroines

Exceptional women in a prosaic male world

Part 3: Her Entirely Modern Views

New and novel takes on the stories

Part 4: Her Beautiful Mind

Worlds of thought, within and beyond the books

Introduction

Happy Birthday, George Eliot

Paul Davies

How do you celebrate a person's 200th birthday? More particularly – how do you celebrate when that person happens to be George Eliot?

Especially when you've been in love with her for over half a century yourself.

I love her playfulness and humour (and, yes, she deserves more credit for both); her unrelenting focus on the role and position of women in society; her honesty with herself; her entirely real and humanly fallible characters; some of her more lovable characters – thinking particularly of Fred and Mary in *Middlemarch*; even the paradoxes to be found in the life of Marian Evans, the amazing woman who became George Eliot – a life apparently so scandalous and yet conducted with such a high moral intent.

Her novels will surprise you. Eliot was firmly committed to being a novelist who reveals ordinary life without needing sensationalism but who has at least two murder trials, one woman saved in the nick of time from being hanged, an exotic and mysterious princess, a step-daughter who turns out to be a major heiress, a banker who is guilty of fraud, a lawyer guilty of worse, and a man who doesn't know his own origins. (All of course pretty commonplace in my village of Goring on Thames in Oxfordshire, but possibly not necessarily common or garden events in most places.)

I've had such pleasure over the years reading her novels and been fascinated by the ideas that she explores.

I wanted to share that feeling and the best way I could think of doing that was helping more people enjoy her novels and that's what this book is all about.

John Walter Cross, who married George Eliot shortly before her death in 1880, published his biography of George Eliot in 1885, where he presented this sparkling woman as some sort of ersatz Queen-Victoria-with-a-brain forever weighed down by the seriousness of her demeanour. In the process the real George Eliot was rather forgotten.

All of our articles in this collection are a tribute to the real person and reveal her and her writing in a new light..

Yes George Eliot was a great thinker, highly intellectual and extraordinarily well read – but she was also a person with a wicked sense of humour and just such a brilliant and tolerant insight into human nature.

She won't appeal to everyone – but it would be great if more people changed from thinking that *they* **ought** *to read* **Middlemarch** to picking it up and immersing themselves in a world apparently so far from our own, but so recognisable on a human level.

In my last year as an undergraduate, I had entered the library with real foreboding carrying my 900 page copy of *Daniel Deronda*, about which I knew nothing.

(Actually only 863 pages of text but 40 pages of notes. That still didn't seem inviting.)

Why the foreboding?

At age 14, at the suggestion of my English teacher, I had tried to read *Silas Marner* – and been baffled by it, bored by it, and generally put off George Eliot for life.

Then in that library I read the first words of *Daniel Deronda* and I was hooked for life:

> Was she beautiful or not beautiful? And what was the secret form or expression which gave the dynamic quality to her glance? Was the good or the evil genius dominant in those beams? Probably the evil . . .

The next two days passed in absolute pleasure and bizarrely I immediately knew what I wanted to write my PhD on – and was in the enviable position of having all her other novels to read.

And my obsession with George Eliot started.

Later to come to me was learning about: the literary critics who disparaged *Daniel Deronda* for all sorts of reasons, not least because she had *gone mad about the Jews*; the absolute brilliance of her mind; the depth of thought; the view that she was too ugly for words; the sheer humanity that she translated onto the page; moments of true pathos; and not least the emotional depth she creates for her readers.

I don't think I've laughed out loud reading her novels, although they can be highly amusing, but I do admit there have been real tears.

The best writing about literature can uncover fresh thoughts and ideas, and undiscovered references. It can bring to life new aspects of the writer's works and add immeasurably to the pleasure of reading – and convey the enthusiasm and engagement with the works.

So what better way to celebrate the 200th anniversary of her life than to stimulate more people to read her wonderful novels?

I therefore asked a range of enthusiastic writers on George Eliot's fiction from all across the world to write short articles revealing and explaining their passion for reading her works, giving us all greater insights into what she accomplished.

I asked them all to avoid as much as possible a dry old academic style and footnotes and references – and write in a conversational tone that is readily accessible, focusing on why an ordinary educated reader would get as much pleasure from the books as we all do. At the same time enhancing the experience of reading the books with insights that will intrigue that reader.

More than one I approached was rather daunted by that – but they've all accepted the challenge and have risen to it brilliantly.

We all hope you will enjoy finding out all the reasons why George Eliot is a writer for grown-ups, why she is actually important as a literary figure – and, most of all, why you have to read the novels for their pure enjoyment.

And just as much, I hope you enjoy reading these articles as much as I have – and feel the same stimulus to read (or re-read) George Eliot's novels.

And I envy everyone who is going to read them for the first time!

So if you have always felt that you *ought* to read *Middlemarch*, I hope this volume will make you *want to*.

This small book is therefore our joint birthday present to George Eliot, born Mary Anne Evans, and known variously as Marian, Mrs M E Lewes, Marian Lewes, Mrs John W Cross – and, by at least one of her major biographers, Polly.

The Articles in this Collection

Charlotte Fiehn asks an important question: why do we still refer to Mary Anne Evans as George Eliot? Looking behind the pseudonym, she explores how it continues to complicate the relationship between the author and her readers.

Sara Håkansson writes about George Eliot's humour, something that has largely been ignored by modern critics, but which is sometimes subtle, often quite wicked, and present in unlikely places.

Sarah Barnette goes a step further and argues that Eliot's humourless image dates to 1885, when her husband, John Walter Cross, published her posthumous "autobiography"—and eliminated all the playfulness and sardonic, at times acidic, humour that runs through her novels and letters.

Cathy Tempelsman has written a play based on Eliot's life (*A Most Dangerous Woman*) and finds surprising parallels in the radical work of Marian Evans (the real George Eliot) and Phoebe Waller-Bridge, of *Fleabag* fame. Both women, she argues, go behind the veneer of polite society to explore transgressive feelings and unsettling truths about female sexuality.

Brenda McKay takes a fascinating look at how George Eliot treated female artists in *The Mill on the Floss* and *Daniel Deronda* in particular. She draws striking parallels with Eliot's own carefully implied experience as a writer – and an outsider. Particularly focused on *The Mill on the Floss* and *Daniel Deronda*,

McKay will make you think about the role of women in stark terms.

Katharine Williams takes a highly personal and deeply affecting perspective on *Janet's Repentance*, from *Scenes of Clerical* Life, and shows how George Eliot transcends stereotypes and common 19th Century attitudes towards mental health in her depiction of an alcoholic woman struggling with an abusive husband, making the work still relevant to us today.

Mari Seaword really engages with *The Mill on the Floss* and reveals how this deeply passionate novel is like a spiritual autobiography of Marian Evans and how it focuses on the dilemmas that unfold in both Maggie and Marian's life.

Angela Runciman shows how important *Middlemarch* has been in her life, both private and academic. Her own relationship with George Eliot becomes the basis for her arguing the importance of women mentoring women to break through any glass ceilings – while remaining hopeful in the process.

Constance Fulmer explores a little-discussed aspect of George Eliot's profound understanding of human relationships and looks at the way Eliot deals with same-sex attraction in a sober, non-judgmental and remarkably modern way.

Dr Ailsa Boyd starts with an intriguing idea – about how the houses that Eliot describes in her novels are indications about the inner life of her characters – and shows how the various interiors are further vivid illustrations of the interplay between the characters and even give us clues about their moral standing.

Akiko Higuchi considers George Eliot's earliest piece of writing, *Edward Neville* (1834), which she wrote at the age of 14, and suggests it is far more than a fragment. Even at that young age, Mary Anne Evans was meticulous in her research of William Coxe's travel book, *An Historical Tour in Monmouthshire* (1801), from which she borrowed a great amount, and yet created an engaging little piece of fiction.

Kathleen McCormack writes about the addiction in the novels, particularly Silas Marner. She suggests that addictive are rather more than just opium and alcohol—and wryly points out why *Silas Marner* itself is not addictive.

Bob Muscutt writes about why he thinks *Adam Bede* is her most impressive novel and focuses on two reasons: the social range of characters and the way that Eliot, by effortlessly fusing location, character, and plot, is almost subliminally both novelist and historian.

Margaret D Stetz brings to life how *The Mill on the Floss* has, over the years, been quite astonishingly abridged and adapted for children – and, more importantly, how the passion and sexuality in Eliot's own life have been obscured for audiences of all ages.

Shinsuke Hori looks at the spread of George Eliot's fame to the ends of the earth – including Japan – and explores how her writing is the best spur to reading literature – any literature – because Eliot always gets to the heart of her characters and is so engaged with both human nature and nature itself.

Catherine Brown engages with *Daniel Deronda*, the only novel that Eliot set relatively close to the time of writing, and reveals how it is the most forward thinking and challenging of her books, covering a wider social range and also a wider range of human nastiness. From there, Brown suggests that we can work out where Eliot would have stood on the debate about Brexit.

David Taylor looks at George Eliot's celebrity in the context of her times – examining her writing through the prism of *Positivism* – and the influence she had, and why Vernon Lushington said that *Adam Bede* was the only novel he had read when it is scarcely true.

Paul Davies looks at the way in which George Eliot creates an entire society's back story in each of her novels, and examines her use of the UK's land laws to create depth and continuity, particularly in *Felix Holt* and *Daniel Deronda*. Those land laws inform the plots but have hardly any actual function other than creating a sense of a complete society, making her characters more understandable.

John Rignall illuminates our reading of the novels by discussing how George Eliot was influenced by German literature – and so much of European culture– and how this gave added depth to her writing.

Shoshana Milgram Knapp focuses on the way that George Eliot posed such difficult moral questions for her characters, and how honestly and bravely she answers them – with neither fear nor favour towards her characters.

Eri Satoh appreciates the way George Eliot's passionate writing opened up a whole new world for her personally – and altered her ambitions – because of the way Eliot captures human nature and places it within a society.

Ben Moore celebrates the *everyday* in George Eliot's novels – focusing on *Middlemarch* but drawing on 'Amos Barton' too, and on the art of Breughel. He illuminates how the everyday needn't actually be inconsequential and how Eliot embraces failure, pain, sadness and disappointment for her characters, but without ever giving up on the humour of daily life. He also teasingly looks at the various ways we might respond to the title, *Middlemarch*, by reflecting on the various meanings of both *middle* and *march*.

Then finally in a short valedictory note, we invite you, our reader, to continue the discussion – and email us with your views and reactions.

Part 1

Her Remarkable Modern Life

How Mary Anne Evans (the Future George Eliot) Still Shocks and Surprises

Chapter 1

George Eliot – Behind the Mask

Charlotte Fiehn

Who was George Eliot?

Approaching this question, and attempting to answer it, is more complicated than you might think. If you're reading this book, you probably already know that George Eliot was not a man. Yet, this is still one of the first points of fact that people have to grapple with when they think about who or what George Eliot was.

Starting with the facts: George Eliot was one of the most successful novelists of the nineteenth century. She was the author of novels, short stories, and poetry. In 1859, she caused a sensation with the publication of *Adam Bede*, a run-away success. She was so successful thereafter that, for example, in 1861, she received the sum of seven thousand pounds, nearly £1m in today's money, from Cornhill Magazine for her novel, *Romola*. From 1871 to 1872, the serial publication of *Middlemarch* secured her reputation as one of the greatest novelists, the novel being, in the opinion of Virginia Woolf, "one of the few...written for grown up people."

None of these facts get us behind the mask, though, and it is striking to think that they are still the main sorts of details that people have in mind when the think of George Eliot. Readers of George Eliot may not know the particulars about *Adam Bede's* publication or the size of the *Romola* paycheck, but they do know (we are almost constantly reminded) that she was one of the major novelists, that *Middlemarch*, in particular, is a major novel and a must-read masterpiece like *War and Peace*. It certainly makes it up there to most lists of top 100 best books ever or top 50 books to read in your lifetime.

All of this raises the question that much more aggressively: why is it that we still know George Eliot by her pseudonym?

People use pseudonyms even today. J.K. Rowling goes by Robert Galbraith when she writes outside of the Harry Potter series. You can make that case even that her choice of "J.K." rather than Joanna Rowling is also something of a disguise, achieving the same effect as a pseudonym by concealing her gender and perhaps also lending an added dash of authority and mystery to her authorial position.

There are other contemporary examples, and it is not difficult to appreciate that pseudonyms were all the more common in the nineteenth century. The difference is that few women hold on to them as George Eliot has. George Sand – a writer with whom Eliot was often compared – is one of the few exceptions but she is also, like Eliot, a very notable exception.

Eliot's exceptionality is also particularly problematic and multidimensional.

Eliot was one of the most successful English novelists of the nineteenth century. She was one of the most influential thinkers of her day, and one of the most insightful commentators of it. Yet, in one sense at least, George Eliot is merely a guise and a fabrication. Today, we might even call her a myth, maintaining our complicated relationship with the writer behind it.

The woman behind the mask, born Mary Ann Evans (later Marian Evans, later Marian Lewes, and Mary Ann Cross) remains something of an enigma. Labelled a "strong-minded woman" by Thomas Carlyle – and this was no compliment at the time – Evans repeatedly defied the conventions of the Victorian period and undeniably escaped the confines of the life she was born. She spent most of her teenage years immersed in a morally stringent brand of evangelicalism, only to reject organized religion in her twenties. Forced into the compromise of attending church but believing what she liked when her father threatened to disown her, Eliot continued to care for Robert Evans until his death and, in her spare time, she translated a major, radical text by a contemporary German philosopher, David Strauss, *The Life of Christ, Critically Examined*.

After the death of her father in 1849, and following a nine-month stint in Geneva, Eliot changed her name from Mary Ann to Marian and moved to London, into a boarding house at 142 Strand, owned by enigmatic publisher, John Chapman. When Chapman acquired the once-celebrated journal, *The Westminster Review*, in 1851, he hired Eliot as the editor-in-chief in all but name, firmly establishing her as a journalist and critic, and she got to rub shoulders with London's literati of the mid-Victorian period.

Much of this detail, strangely, is now forgotten by all but the most ardent enthusiasts for her life and those who study her. There is, perhaps surprisingly, a quite singular reason for this.

The most defining moment in the life of Marian Evans came in 1854: at thirty-five years old, Evans chose to establish a relationship with fellow writer, George Henry Lewes, who happened to be married with no hope of divorce.

Now, the particulars of Victorian divorce law are decidedly complicated, and there is still debate about whether divorce would even have been an option for Lewes. When he met Marian, it was almost certainly impossible and there would have been no hope of remarriage. In 1857, a new law was passed to make divorce slightly easier, but it was still decidedly costly and potentially very public and embarrassing for all parties. Adultery was really the only grounds reason for divorce and Lewes's wife Agnes had had at least one child by her lover (and Lewes's erstwhile friend) Thornton Leigh Hunt. But Lewes had also committed adultery and if he was seen to have condoned his wife's affair that would have complicated matters even further. At some point it was decided that even attempting to obtain a divorce was pointless. It is perhaps worth adding that Agnes Lewes apparently had no objections to her husband's liaison with Evans, which lasted for the rest of his life. (Later in life, Evans was also a very active step-mother to Lewes's children).

Circumstances were of little importance, however, to Victorian society. The decision to live openly with a married man, whatever the circumstances, led to social exclusion for the woman. Evans was dubbed the "other woman" and a "fallen woman." She was excluded from polite society for most of the rest of her life and it is primarily because of her status as a "fallen woman" that Marian Lewes became George Eliot when she decided to write fiction.

Eliot's was undoubtedly an authorial identity created out of necessity.

Like the Brontës, who also recognized the tendency for critics to judge novels based on the gender of their authors, Evans realized that she would be at a considerable disadvantage if she published her work with an open acknowledgement of her identity. She wrote an essay very much to this effect in 1856 entitled "Silly Novels by Lady Novelists."

But she not only needed a male pseudonym to nurture her critical reputation, she needed to maintain the secrecy of her identity. And so George Eliot was created circa 1857, to enable the publication of *Scenes of Clerical Life*. The ruse didn't last, though, and it is important to any consideration of Eliot's authorial identity to have some sense of exactly how and to what extent Eliot was eventually unmasked.

Such was the phenomenon of Eliot's first novel *Adam Bede* in 1859, that there was not only rampant speculation about her identity but a substantial forgery case, with one particularly determined individual writing out the entirety of Adam Bede in a bid to claim credit. The forgery case in particular forced Eliot's hand and Lewes cautiously arranged for Blackwood to be introduced to Marian as Eliot.

From that point on, it became increasingly widely known exactly who Eliot was – at least within certain important circles.

The remarkable thing thereafter is that she almost weathered the inevitable storm. Her popular and critical success meant that she was very nearly or at least tentatively rehabilitated – almost able to cast off the guise of the "fallen woman." One particularly striking anecdote in this story is the occasion on which one of Queen Victoria's daughters broke royal protocol and introduced herself to her favourite author. And for all of these biographical details, Eliot stands as a prime example of an anti-Victorian woman in the best sense, a woman who actively opposed the restrictive values and conventions of the period and overcame them.

There is, however, much weight in *almost* when it comes to Evans's story and her apparent social triumph. On the one hand, she was a phenomenally successful writer. On the other, she was a woman disowned by her brother and denied access to her extended family because of her relationship with a married man. She was a woman who defied convention throughout her life, but her social position left her excluded from most of society and, crucially, unable to speak out in her own voice.

Many feminist critics have looked to Evans expecting to find the evidence of her proto-feminism overwhelming. Evans's recorded opinions on issues such as woman's suffrage – this being the hot topic of the nineteenth century –dash most such expectations. She also resisted pressure to engage in popular reform movements, including efforts to secure women's suffrage. She did not openly advocate for women to have the vote, although she counted among her friends many who did. She publicly supported women's education, donating to Girton College, which she visited, but these contributions might be thought meagre in light of her wealth and she never advocated for these rights in a public forum.

Reports of her conservativism are exaggerated, with many confusing public reticence and reserve with outright disapproval, but Evans clearly had reasons to keep her opinions private, and it is something people too often forget. In a letter written in 1878, Evans explained that she had "grave reasons for not speaking on certain public topics" (quoted in Thomas 393). Although she went on to describe aesthetic reasons why she avoided expressing her opinions openly, some of this public conservativism and reticence traces to her position as a "fallen" and "strong-minded" woman.

Although modern attitudes and mores lead many to believe that a woman might as well be outspoken when outcast, the reality for Mary Ann Evans – and presumably for any woman in her situation – was an inevitable public condemnation of radical opinions, regardless of how much she might have done to rehabilitate herself in certain circles.

There is also, as a secondary but still important matter, the question of what to call her if not Eliot. Should we refer to her as Mary Ann Evans, the name she was born (and christened) with? Should we go with the French version of her name, Marian, which she adopted after her stay in Geneva? Should we drop Evans and go with the name she used for most of her life, Marian Lewes, acknowledging her partnership with George Lewes as central? Or should we go with name she was buried with: Marian Cross? A name that – acquired because of her marriage to John Cross in 1879 –bought her sufficient respectability to put her back in touch with the brother who disowned her?

That these questions (as much as the first) remain unanswered, is evidence, I feel, that Marian Evans continues to be excluded. The guise of George Eliot remains a necessary fixture for her reputation, because to confront the woman behind it is to embrace complexity and the enduring scandal of a nineteenth century woman.

About the Contributor

Charlotte Fiehn is a PhD student at the University of Texas-Austin, specializing in nineteenth and early twentieth century British and American literature, particularly the writings of George Eliot and Virginia Woolf. She completed her undergraduate degree at the University of Cambridge.

She has published articles on Shakespeare, George Eliot, and Charlotte Brontë. She has also contributed book chapters on Henry James, Joseph Conrad, and George Eliot.

Her current research addresses questions of form and gender in the works of George Eliot and Virginia Woolf and she recently won the 2019 George Eliot Fellowship Essay Prize for her essay on water symbolism in *Romola*.

Chapter 2

Humour in George Eliot's Commentary

Sara Håkansson

The first time I laughed out loud while reading George Eliot was at a scene in *Middlemarch* when Dorothea Brooke's rejected suitor Sir James Chettam gossips with Mrs Cadwallader about Dorothea's engagement to the much older Edward Casaubon. Mrs Cadwallader breaks the news to Chettam who responds:

> 'Good God! It is horrible! He is no better than a mummy!' /.../
> 'She says, he is a great soul.— A great bladder for dried peas to rattle in!' said Mrs Cadwallader.
> 'What business has an old bachelor like that to marry?' said Sir James. 'He has one foot in the grave.'
> 'He means to draw it out again, I suppose' (*Middlemarch*, vi, 54).

The scene is one example of many where George Eliot demonstrates her great sense of humour as well as her ability to create characters that are timelessly identifiable and recognisable. We all know a Mrs Cadwallader, and if we do not know one, we can recognise the type.

Similarly, we might know a Mr Casaubon, whose foot is about to be drawn out of the grave by the grace of a much younger wife. Eliot's novels are riddled with these recognisable types, not seldom female characters who take on the role of ancient choruses to comment on events, characters or circumstances in the narrative.

In the *Mill on the Floss*, this chorus is referred to as the "World's Wife" – a specifically female community chorus which administers reproof and spreads rumours. It is as moralistic as it is hypocritical and the humour lies in the paradox.

The view of George Eliot's humour – is she funny or not – has undergone some change since the late nineteenth century. Her contemporary readers certainly did not question her humour but rather considered it central to the understanding of her novels.[1] Yet, the prevailing perception of Eliot since her death has been to associate her novels with profound wisdom, moralism and a keen sense of dignity. If there is humour, it rather prompts the mouth to twitch at the corners than triggers a belly laugh.

Gordon Haight ascribes this general impression to John Walter Cross whom Eliot married shortly before she died in 1880. Cross edited out most humorous content from Eliot's letters and generally worked to promote her image as a serious writer.[2] Patricia Shaw suggests that the modern reader's impression of Eliot could be influenced by the strong evangelical

---

[1] Indeed, in 1871 the anthology *Wise, Witty and Tender Sayings in Prose and Verse, Selected from the Works of George Eliot*, was collected by Alexander Main and published by Blackwood with Eliot's approval. See also R. J. Jenkins' article from 2006, "Laughing with George Eliot" in *The George Eliot Review*, 2006; 37: 36-45.

[2] Haight, Gordon, S., ed., *The George Eliot Letters, 9 vols* (New Haven: Yale University Press, 1954-78).

orientation of her youth.[3] Before writing any prose she translated two deeply religious German works (F. F. Strauss' *Life of Jesus*, 1846 and L. Feuerbach's *Essence of Christianity*, 1854), the gravity of which may eclipse any sense of humour or wit in the translator.

Whatever the reason for thinking of Eliot as a serious, almost dreary, author, the comedy of characters such as Mrs Cadwallader above or the Tulliver and Dodson aunts in *The Mill on the Floss* (likened to hens), or even Amos Barton's maid in *Scenes of Clerical Life*, serve to convey a different perspective into the narrative worlds that Eliot creates, which is all but dull. The humour of these characters and many more add to a comprehensive understanding of the novels as wholes as well as to our understanding of George Eliot as a person and an author.

Accordingly, there are numerous characters throughout Eliot's oeuvre that cause readers to laugh. But Eliot is humorous even when she steps away from the narrative world and addresses the reader directly.

Instances of narratorial commentary in the novels, as understood as moments when the narrator calls attention to his or her voice, are generally associated with the narrator's attempts at eliciting sympathy from the reader. These comments appeal to the reader's understanding by endeavouring to stimulate the reader's sense of recognition. If we recognise and can relate to situations or scenarios, we are more likely to sympathise with them. Indeed, in one of Eliot's most famous quotes she states that the "only effect I ardently long to produce by my writings, is that those who read

---

[3] Shaw, Patricia, "Humour in the Novels of George Eliot", *Filologia Moderna* (Madrid, Spain) 1973; 13: 305.

them should be better able to *imagine* and *feel* the pains and the joys of those who differ from themselves".[4]

However, recognition can also serve to highlight the comical and in several of Eliot's narratorial comments, the narrator operates almost like a stand-up comedian pointing to the humorous in recognisable situations. For example, commenting on Adam's inability to see through Hetty Sorrel's beauty (and see her for what she really is) the narrator of *Adam Bede* reflects:

> Long dark eyelashes, now—what can be more exquisite? I find it impossible not to expect some depth of soul behind a deep grey eye with a long dark eyelash, in spite of an experience which has shown me that they may go along with deceit, peculation, and stupidity. But if, in the reaction of disgust, I have betaken myself to a fishy eye, there has been a surprising similarity of result. One begins to suspect at length that there is no direct correlation between eyelashes and morals; or else, that the eyelashes express the disposition of the fair one's grandmother, which is on the whole less important to us
> *(Adam Bede*, xv, 154)

Like many young men in similar situations before and after, Adam is mesmerised by Hetty's beauty and for that, he is tenderly mocked. But there are interesting layers at work here. In *Adam Bede*, Eliot assumes a male narrator and her pseudonym has not yet been revealed by the workings of the dishonest, but poverty stricken, Joseph Liggins who took credit for her early work. Hence, the comment emanates from a male

---

[4] Haight, Gordon, S., ed., The George Eliot Letters, 9 vols (New Haven: Yale University Press, 1954-78), iii, 111.

narrator, created by what most contemporary readers (except for Charles Dickens) believed was a male author.

Initially, the comment seems to address a male audience, appealing to readers with reflections they are assumed to recognise; but underneath this recognition the irony undermines its very basis and reverses the perspective so that it is the narrator himself, as a representative of a ridiculous tendency, who is satirised. And, yet, underneath these layers of satire and irony, we can picture Marian Evans, smiling like the Mona Lisa at the scenario she has created and the digs she manages to subtly dish out.

There are several examples of humorous narratorial commentary, though, that manage to combine the narrator's appeal for sympathy with humour. In *Felix Holt, the Radical*, Eliot describes the lawyer, Matthew Jermyn in a hilarious account:

> A German poet was entrusted with a particularly fine sausage, which he was to convey to the donor's friend at Paris. In the course of a long journey he smelled the sausage; he got hungry, and desired to taste it; he pared a morsel off, then another, and another, in successive moments of temptation, till at last the sausage was, humanly speaking, at an end. The offence had not been premeditated. The poet had never loved meanness, but he loved sausage; and the result was undeniably awkward.
> So it was with Matthew Jermyn
> (*Felix Holt*, ix, 99).

What reader has not, tempted by something particularly suited to the palate, told themselves they will just have one small piece – and then another – and then another? Matthew Jermyn is not an especially sympathetic character and yet Eliot here nuances the reader's understanding of him. He may be dodgy, but through the comical account, we are invited to understand how his particular flaws have evolved – flaws, which we may excuse in our own selves.

Patricia Shaw claims that Eliot is "a more acute observer of human nature" than any of her contemporaries. Indeed, observation is an essential part of her humour and as we laugh at characters and scenes, we also laugh at ourselves and the comical aspects of human nature.

This is one of the greatest lessons George Eliot has taught me.

In my early days as a young academic, I was preoccupied with being taken seriously and positioning myself in a competitive profession. In this endeavour, I gradually lost my sense of fun and the ability to reconcile serious business with enjoyment – that which had brought me to literature in the first place. Now, some thirty years later, after having revisited Eliot innumerable times, I realise that on a subconscious level, she has not only restored my sense of enjoyment for fiction – I am allowed to have fun as I read – but she has also served as a role model. She is intelligent, astute, observant of human nature, well aware of the goods and evils in the world and nonetheless, she manages to be funny. Additionally, every time I read an Eliot novel, I see and learn something new.

My final example serves as a timely lesson in humility.

Having taught English literature for a number of years, I found myself walking into classes with a near arrogant confidence in my own pedagogical skills and the impression I could make on students. The fact that they often left the classroom having said very little, I put down to a respectful veneration for the university experience, feeling certain that they, nevertheless, had been captivated by the knowledge communicated. But at one point, when I re-read *The Mill on the Floss*, a particular narratorial comment spoke to me. It refers to Tom Tulliver's private lessons with his uncle Pullet but contains a general truth about the relationship between teachers and students that hit home:

> A boy's sheepishness is by no means a sign of overmastering reverence; and while you are making encouraging advances to him under the idea that he is overwhelmed by a sense of your age and wisdom, ten to one he is thinking you extremely queer. The only consolation I can suggest to you is, that the Greek boys probably thought the same of Aristotle
>
> (*The Mill on the Floss*, ix, 91).

So it is, of course, that for some students, my ravings about George Eliot's genius probably render me peculiar in their view.

I do take consolation in the narrator's presumption that Aristotle's students felt the same, but primarily I take consolation in the fact that if I can reach one student it is well worth seeming odd to the rest. And I believe that reflecting on George Eliot's humour and irony is an effective way of reaching that one student, and preferably more.

By allowing ourselves as readers to actually see and feel Eliot's humour, we also allow ourselves to experience her narrative worlds more comprehensively as well as a little more similarly to the way her contemporaries did. They understood that fine balance between laughter and gravity in which the impact of something read has its force.

By laughing with George Eliot, I believe, so will we.

Bibliography:

Eliot, George, *Adam Bede*, Oxford World's Classics, ed. by Valentine Cunningham (Oxford: Oxford University Press, 1996)

Eliot, George, *Felix Holt, the Radical*, Oxford World's Classics, ed. by Fred C. Thomson (Oxford: Oxford University Press, 1988)

Eliot, George, *Middlemarch: A Study of Provincial Life*, Oxford World's Classics, ed. by David Carroll (Oxford: Oxford University Press, 1997)

Eliot, George, *The Mill on the Floss*, Oxford World's Classics, ed. by Gordon S. Haight (Oxford University Press, 1996)

Eliot, George, *Scenes of Clerical Life*, Oxford World's Classics, ed. by Thomas A. Noble (Oxford: Oxford University Press, 1988)

Haight, Gordon, S., ed., *A Century of George Eliot Criticism* (London: Methuen, 1965)

Haight, Gordon, S., ed., *The George Eliot Letters, 9 vols* (New Haven: Yale University Press, 1954-78).

Jenkins, R. J., 'Laughing with George Eliot' in *The George Eliot Review: Journal of the George Eliot Fellowship*, 37 (2006), 36-45

Shaw, Patricia, 'Humour in the Novels of George Eliot' in, *Filologia Moderna*, 13 (1973), 305-335

About the Contributor

Sara Håkansson holds a PhD in English literature from Lund University. Her thesis, *Narratorial Commentary in George Eliot's Novels,* was published in 2009 and since then she has worked on various projects related to George Eliot, the latest being "The Function of Dogs in George Eliot's Fiction" published in the bicentennial collection *George Eliot: Interdisciplinary Essays* edited by Jean Arnold and Lila Harper in 2019.

She is currently involved in a research project which studies aspects of the visual in George Eliot's novels with a particular focus on the significance of the visual in relation to characterisation.

Chapter 3

George Eliot:
Rude, Wry, Cynical and Fun

Sarah Barnette

Last winter I found a small ornate card prettily framed in an antique shop. It had elaborate scrollwork in red ink surrounding a quotation attributed to George Eliot: 'What matter then where your feet stand, or wherewith your hands are busy, so that it is the spot where God has put you, and the work which He has given you to do'.

The quotation was so solemn, so dutiful – so dull – so very unlike the arch and mischievous George Eliot I know that I bought it, convinced it came more from the posthumous image we have been given of Eliot as conservative sibyl-on-a-soapbox than her actual self.

And it did.

The line is not George Eliot's at all. It was printed in a collection entitled *The Value of Contentment* published in 1911 by a Mary Minerva Barrows as one of many passages meditating on contentment as a virtue. Barrows attributes it to Eliot, but it is, in fact, from *Faith Gartney's Girlhood* (1863), a religious novel by the American writer A.D.T. (Adeline Dutton Train) Whitney (1824–1906) who was known for her conventional themes aimed – of all things – at keeping girls and young women submissively in the home.

How did such a slip happen? Why is our most readily available picture of Eliot so (excruciatingly) austere that the words of an evangelical writer can be mistaken for hers?

The wholly serious and moralizing image we have been handed down of George Eliot is not her true image. She was also snide and impish; she was subversive; she misbehaved; she could be rude, wry and cynical, self-deprecating and critical with a keen eye for the preposterousness in herself and others – and often it was all for the simple sake of having a good laugh.

In short, to forget about (or ignore) the humorous side of Eliot is to misapprehend her altogether.

It seems that we have not been allowed to think of Eliot as funny for a long time.[1] This trend can be attributed in large part to Eliot's widower John Walter Cross and to his *Life of George Eliot* (1885). Cross edited Eliot's letters and journals for his biography of her to such an extent that he 'created a George Eliot who never really existed, a marmoreal image' and 'legend of lofty seriousness' that have persisted into the twenty-first century.[2]

To get the flavour of Cross's *Life*, we need look no further than a few contemporary reactions. The politician William Gladstone (1809–1898) called it 'a reticence in three volumes', while the writer Eliza Lynn Linton (1822–1898) sneered at it as 'a trimmed, erased,

---

[1] R.J. Rifkins gives us a thoughtful history of the reasons for this in 'Laughing with George Eliot', *George Eliot Review* 37 (2006), pp. 36-45. <http://georgeeliotreview.org/items/show/632>. Accessed 25 September 2019.

[2] Gordon S. Haight, 'Preface', *The George Eliot Letters*, 9 vols., edited by Gordon S. Haight (New Haven, CT: Yale University Press, 1978), I, ix-xvi (p. xv).

and amended protocol. In a word, the book has been written to embalm and preserve the image of the Ideal George Eliot'.[3]

Alice James (1848–1892), Henry James's sister, called it 'a monument of ponderous dreariness' in which Eliot's 'dank, moaning features haunt and pursue one thro' the book'. 'What a lifeless, diseased, self-conscious being she must have been! Not one burst of joy, not one ray of humour'.[4] Yikes.

There was likely such express disappointment over the tedium of Cross's *Life* because while alive Eliot had been so celebrated for her humour. 'George Eliot's brilliant comedy should be most talked about', claimed one reviewer of *Felix Holt, The Radical* (1866).

Another writes, 'in *Adam Bede* there is real humour of a rare and genuine kind'. *Middlemarch* was hailed as 'showing a humour so large and delicate that that laughter which really brightens the spirits breaks out even if we are alone'.

Edith Simcox (1844–1901), ardent Eliot-devotee, praised Eliot's overall ability to 'find [...] much everywhere to laugh at'.[5]

This is the Eliot I know, and a sampler of her letters to friends shows her ability in action:

---

[3] Quoted by Barbara Hardy, *George Eliot: A Critic's Biography* (London: Continuum, 2006), p. 49; quoted by Gordon S. Haight, 'Cross's Biography of George Eliot', *The Yale University Library Gazette* 25:1 (July 1950), 1-9 (p. 2).

[4] Alice James, *The Diary of Alice James*, edited by Leon Edel (Boston: Northeastern University Press, 1999), p 41.

[5] David Carroll (ed.), *George Eliot: The Critical Heritage* (London; New York: Routledge, 1995), pp. 254, 74, 298, 328.

Dear Friends, I have been expecting a letter from you for the last two or three days and I am just now hating you intensely because the postman has just been here and has brought nothing for me.

I am still thin and my hair is falling off – so how much will be left of me by next April I am afraid to imagine. I shall be length without breadth – quite bald and without money to buy a wig.

The Marquise took on her the office of femme de chambre and drest my hair one day. She has abolished all my curls and made two things stick out on each side of my head, like those on the head of the Sphinx. All the world says I look infinitely better so I comply, though to myself I seem uglier than ever – if possible.

I am frightened to think what an idle wretch I am becoming. And you all do not write me one word to tell me you long for me. Your hearts are perfect flint and you have no bowels. I have a great mind to elope to Constantinople and never see any one any more!

Two other young Germans – Prussians – are here – the eldest odious, with an eternal simper and a mouth of dubious cleanliness. He speaks French very little and has a miserable splutter between a grunt and a snuffle so that when he begins to speak to one one's brain begins to twist and one feels inclined to rush out of the room. His brother frowns instead of simpering and is therefore more endurable.

Foxton came, smelling horribly of tobacco, and sat talking with me an hour and a half by the timepiece till I was half dead.

Dr. Hodgson is here, and a Mr. Jarvis, an American, evidently a noodle.

This place is surrounded with trees and does not appear to suit us. But my ailments are of no consequence – they only make me inclined to drown myself. Still I have no doubt I shall survive the temptation and be pretty well to-morrow.

I have little patience with people who can find time to pity Louis Philippe and his moustachioed sons. Certainly our decayed monarchs should be pensioned off: we should have a hospital for them, or a sort of Zoological Garden, where these worn out humbugs may be preserved. It is but justice that we should keep them, since we have spoiled them for any honest trade.[6]

---

[6] George Eliot, *Letters*: I, p. 331, GE to Charles Bray (1 March 1850); I, p. 310, GE to Mr. and Mrs. Charles Bray (20 September 1849); I, p. 298, GE to Mr. and Mrs. Charles Bray and Sara Sophia Hennell (20 August 1849); I, p. 331, GE to Charles Bray (1 March 1850); I, pp. 296-97, GE to Mr. and Mrs. Charles Bray and Sara Sophia Hennell (20 August 1849); I, p. 345, GE to Mr. and Mrs. Charles Bray (15 February 1851); I, p. 341, GE to Mrs. Charles Bray (8 January 1851); I, p. 357, GE to John Chapman (1 August 1851); I, pp. 253-54, GE to John Sibree, Jr., (8 March 1848).

Droll self-deprecation; shameless caricature; soft and whimsical observation; sardonic social criticism: these are Eliot's trademarks just as much as any moralizing – and so often she hits you over the head with them.

Like her letters, Eliot's writing as a journalist is brimming with her sense of fun. Rosemary Ashton notes the 'magnificent malice' in two of Eliot's early essays – 'Evangelical Teaching: Dr Cumming' (1855) and 'Silly Novels by Lady Novelists' (1856) – and they are so deliciously malicious because of her humour.[7]

Each piece addresses a serious topic – truth (or its absence) in religious teaching, and the question of female intelligence in the literary marketplace – and each piece eviscerates its subject with sustained glee. The opening lines of 'Evangelical Teaching' cut as they amuse:

> Given, a man with moderate intellect, a moral standard not higher than the average, some rhetorical affluence and great glibness of speech, what is the career in which, without the aid of birth or money, he may most easily attain power and reputation in English society? Where is that Goshen of mediocrity in which a smattering of science and learning will pass for profound instruction, where platitudes will be accepted as wisdom, bigoted narrowness as holy zeal, unctuous egoism as God-given piety? Let such a man become an evangelical preacher; he will then find it possible to reconcile small ability with great ambition, superficial knowledge with the prestige of erudition, a

---

[7] Rosemary Ashton, *George Eliot: A Life* (Middlesex: Penguin Books, 1997), p. 161.

middling morale with a high reputation for sanctity.[8]

The Rev. John Cumming (1807–1881) was a Scottish clergyman with a penchant for virulent preaching. He was an interpreter of Biblical prophecy and harbinger of the End Times (which he claimed would occur between 1848 and 1867), but in her essay Eliot exposes his message of gloom and doom as absurd. With humour and a little logic, she reduces him to 'a specimen of the astounding ignorance which was possible in a metropolitan preacher, AD 1854'.[9]

Sparks fly, too, when Eliot levels her devastating fun at 'silly lady novelists':

> To judge from their writings, there are certain ladies who think that an amazing ignorance, both of science and of life, is the best possible qualification for forming an opinion on the knottiest moral and speculative questions. Apparently, their recipe for solving all such difficulties is something like this: – Take a woman's head, stuff it with a smattering of philosophy and literature chopped small, and with false notions of society baked hard, let it hang over a desk a few hours every day, and serve up hot in feeble English, when not required.[10]

Food quips and metaphors run throughout this essay. They act collectively like barbs on a wire to lacerate any middle- or upper-class women who are ruining the writing trade for professional ladies. If only they would

---

[8] George Eliot, *Selected Essays, Poems and Other Writings*, edited by A.S. Byatt (London: Penguin Books, 1990), p. 38.
[9] *Selected Essays*, p. 47.
[10] *Selected Essays*, p. 149.

acquire precise skills (like cooking or baking) that would clue them into the causal relationship between a final product and the order, quality, and quantity of ingredients.

The icing on the cake, for me though, is Eliot's description of a specific 'species' of silly novel: 'the *white neck-cloth* species, which represent the tone of thought and feeling in the Evangelical party' and is 'intended as a sort of medicinal sweetmeat for Low Church young ladies'.[11]

My little framed quotation from *Faith Gartney's Girlhood* is, in fact, taken from a sermon delivered by a young 'handsome' and 'broken-hearted' evangelical preacher in the novel. The eponymous heroine as good as swoons after hearing it: 'Faith could not tell what hymn was sung, or what were the words of the prayer that followed the sermon. There was a music and an uplifting in her own soul that made them needless'.[12]

I defer to Eliot: 'the hero is almost sure to be a young curate, frowned upon, perhaps, by worldly mammas, but carrying captive the hearts of their daughters, who can "never forget *that* sermon"'. It would seem that Eliot had the measure of this novel – published seven years after her essay – without ever needing to read it, and she is very clear on her opinion: 'in one particular the novels of the White Neck-cloth School are meritoriously realistic, – their favourite hero, the Evangelical young curate, is always rather an insipid personage'.[13]

---

[11] *Selected Essays*, p.156
[12] A.D.T. Whitney, *Faith Gartney's Girlhood and A Summer in Leslie Goldthwaite's Life* (London: Ward, Lock, and Tyler, 1870), pp. 106-7.
[13] *Selected Essays*, p. 157.

In writing her own fiction, Eliot never missed a beat. She continued to make fun of herself, society, and others.

She is even comic about young women fascinated by clergymen. Eliot's union of the young and idealistic Dorothea Brooke with the aged Rev. Edward Casaubon in *Middlemarch*, for instance, is funny. It smacks of the ludicrous. Consider the exchange between a spellbound Dorothea and her – thoroughly unimpressed – sister Celia following their introduction to Casaubon:

> When the two girls were in the drawing-room alone, Celia said –
> "How very ugly Mr Casaubon is!"
> "Celia! He is one of the most distinguished-looking men I ever saw. He is remarkably like the portrait of Locke. He has the same deep eye-sockets."
> "Had Locke those two white moles with hairs on them?"
> "Oh, I daresay! when people of a certain sort looked at him," said Dorothea, walking away a little.[14]

As a young woman, Eliot (then Mary Ann Evans) had had a similarly baffling fascination with a much older man, a Dr. Robert Brabant with whom she stayed in 1843, and her spry slips into humour where Dorothea and Casaubon are concerned hint at a self-knowing irony even as they also critique a society that keeps young women so poorly educated.[15]

---

[14] George Eliot, *Middlemarch*, edited by Rosemary Ashton (London: Penguins Books, 1994), p. 20.
[15] See Ashton, *George Eliot: A Life*, pp. 47-49, 61 for more on Dr. Brabant.

But you need not know any backstory to laugh with (or at) her characters. We laugh with Mrs. Cadwallader, for instance, who never misses an opportunity to jibe at Casaubon and his dusty scholarship:

> "He has got no good red blood in his body," said Sir James.
> "No. Somebody put a drop under a magnifying-glass, and it was all semicolons and parentheses," said Mrs Cadwallader.[16]

And we laugh at the impressionable Rev. Amos Barton in *Scenes of Clerical Life* when the narrator tells us,

> Now, the Rev. Amos Barton was one of those men who have a decided will and opinion of their own; he held himself bolt upright, and had no self-distrust. He would march very determinedly along the road he thought best; but then it was wonderfully easy to convince him which *was* the best road.[17]

As in her letters, she has fun with people's looks: 'I believe there have been plenty of young heroes, of middle stature and feeble beards, who have felt quite sure they could never love anything more insignificant than a Diana, and yet have found themselves in middle life happily settled with a wife who waddles'.[18]

And with past fashions: 'Mrs Pullet brushed each doorpost with great nicety, [...] (at that period a woman was truly ridiculous to an instructed eye if she

---

[16] *Middlemarch*, pp. 70-71.
[17] George Eliot, *Scenes of Clerical Life*, edited by David Lodge (New York: Penguin Books, 1973), p. 67.
[18] George Eliot, *Adam Bede*, edited by Stephen Gill (New York: Penguin Books, 1980), p. 224.

did not measure a yard and a half across the shoulders)'.[19]

The arch narrator often displays Eliot at her most roguish. In *Middlemarch*, the narrator takes a swipe at the bumbling gentleman landowner Mr. Brooke when he goes into politics, musing that it was 'as if a tortoise of desultory pursuits should protrude its small head ambitiously and become rampant'.[20]

The fresh and lovely Hetty in Adam Bede is compared with 'a young star-browed calf, [...] that, being inclined for a promenade out of bounds, leads you a severe steeple-chase over hedge and ditch, and only comes to a stand in the middle of a bog'.[21]

And the narrator makes fun of us: 'The rooks were cawing with many-voiced monotony, apparently – by a remarkable approximation to human intelligence – finding great conversational resources in the change of weather'.[22]

Even Eliot's serious observations can quickly turn flippant: 'If we had a keen vision and feeling of all ordinary human life, it would be like hearing the grass grow and the squirrel's heart beat, and we should die of that roar which lies on the other side of silence. As it is, the quickest of us walk about well wadded with stupidity'.[23]

Today, we most often see, on the one hand, a readership that knows very little about George Eliot

---

[19] George Eliot, *The Mill on the Floss* (London: Wordsworth Editions Limited, 1995), p. 50.
[20] *Middlemarch*, p. 359.
[21] *Adam Bede*, pp. 128-29.
[22] *Scenes of Clerical Life*, p. 181.
[23] *Middlemarch*, p. 194.

except for some vague notion that 'his' books are cumbersome and dreary and, on the other hand, the ubiquitous stance among literary scholars that Eliot's oeuvre – as a touchstone of nineteenth-century intellectual thought – should be treated like a museum with the period's varying discourses on display.

It is true that Eliot's works are a mine of profound revelations on character and the moral consequences of our actions, and as a literary scholar I value her writing for its dizzying breadth and depth – she truly did seem to know something about everything in a thoroughly exasperating fashion – but I hope I have shown, too, that we do her a disservice by only approaching her work in this way.

Museums are cultural centres for everyone, yes, yet they imply hushed voices and ponderous expressions and the expectation that any fun to be had must be laced with learning. It is really sometimes more accurate (and satisfying) to treat Eliot's texts as places that relish the unexpected turn in meaning, celebrate the rude comment, and luxuriate in unconventional pairings.

In her letters, essays, and novels alike, Eliot plays on our senses of humour like an exquisite harpist on strings, deftly moving up and down the scale from gentle banter to rude joke to caustic comment.

There is plenty of fun to be had in Eliot.

As for my sombre A.D.T. Whitney quotation: I keep it in the kitchen so I can see it when my hands are busy with the dishes – like reading George Eliot, it is always good for a laugh.

About the Contributor

Sarah Barnette earned her M.Litt in Romantic and Victorian Studies at the University of St. Andrews in

2011 and completed her Ph.D in English Literature at the University of Oxford in 2017.

Her interest in Victorian literary ethics and engagement with difference led to her dissertation, 'Many-sided Sympathy & the Science of Religion in George Eliot, Vernon Lee, & Edna Lyall'. Sarah is ambitious about revitalizing George Eliot's image for a new generation of readers.

She received the University of Oxford's Knowledge Exchange Seed Fund in partnership with the George Eliot Fellowship in 2015-16 for the project 'George Eliot's England'. She is a co-founder of *Humanities of the World*, a public engagement project that aims to promote the value of the humanities.

Chapter 4

"...earthly sensual and devilish": Lifting the Veil on George Eliot's Modern Life and Legacy

Cathy Tempelsman

Fans of Phoebe Waller-Bridge couldn't wait for Season 2 of *Fleabag*, the hit series based on her solo show at the Edinburgh Fringe. In just a few years, Waller-Bridge has become as popular and well known in the U.S. as in the U.K. Early critics, however, weren't quite sure what to make of her.

The Telegraph praised the writer's "keen ear for how people actually speak" and a woman's right to be "unlikeable." But the reviewer found her narcissism "wearisome."

The Times called the piece "gleefully filthy." As to the meaning of Waller-Bridge's honest, explicit monologue, the critic drew a blank.

I confess to being somewhat shocked by the first episode. But my shock gave way to a sense of déjà vu: a young woman creating flawed characters...an honest, unvarnished view of women's lives and sexuality...a fascination with secret, transgressive feelings...

And then it hit me.

I've studied George Eliot for years (my play *A Most Dangerous Woman* is based on her remarkable life), and I was struck by the similarities between two writers who, on the surface, have little in common. But the parallels are there.

Both George Eliot and Phoebe Waller-Bridge are deeply committed to truth in art. Both women confounded early critics with a highly original, even scandalous take on real life. And neither anticipated the cult-like devotion that would follow—though one remains in the shadow of a male pseudonym.

Writing nearly two centuries apart, each 30-something writer took a deep dive beneath the veneer of polite society. In *Fleabag*, Waller-Bridge explores feelings that women *still* feel compelled to hide. Her characters, like Eliot's, are ordinary and deeply flawed. Her heroines do and say the unspeakable. They are also startlingly real in their humanity.

And both writers speak to their audience with an honesty—an intimacy—that is almost electric.

Every time Phoebe Waller-Bridge looks into the camera and addresses us directly, I think of Eliot's wise, knowing narrator (she has always felt to me like the older sister I never had), and who often interrupts her story to speak directly to readers. I'm reminded that Eliot's bold experiment in realism is very much alive.

My gift to the writer on her 200th birthday? Some of the credit she deserves for a truly modern legacy.

A Spinster Escapes

Even as a child, the precocious Mary Anne Evans (the future George Eliot's name at birth) stood out for her intelligence. But she was also notoriously homely. And in a society that valued beauty above all in a woman, this would prove decisive.

For fifteen years she kept house for her pious father. As she grew, her magnificent brain would act as a magnet in attracting men. But it couldn't compensate for a lack of beauty: no man, it seemed, would love her.

At 29, she nursed Robert Evans through a final illness. And then, the night before he died, Mary Ann (she got rid of that 'e' at the end of her name) wrote in a letter:

> What shall I be without my father? It will seem as if a part of my moral nature were gone. I had a horrid vision of myself last night becoming earthly sensual and devilish for want of that purifying restraining influence.

"Earthly." "Sensual." "Devilish." Even today, I find those words shocking! Many scholars note the letter dismissively, if at all. I suppose this image doesn't accord with the mature, literary icon who wrote *Middlemarch*.

But no one chose words more carefully than Mary Ann Evans, and she clearly felt untethered. Philip Davis, a recent biographer, refers to the 'sexual chaos' inside her. In a Christian, pre-Freudian society, such feelings in a woman could only mean that she was evil. She was terrified of what she might do—and for good reason.

After her father's death, the family wanted her to live with a sister and tutor the children. Instead, she renamed herself Marian (the woman had more names than Hillary Clinton once had hairdos) and fled to London. There she thrived intellectually. But for all her success, she still craved love and affection. And still no man would have her.

Until George Henry Lewes came along.

Lewes was eccentric and irreverent. He was also brilliant, funny, and a stunning polymath. He wrote books on ancient philosophy and Goethe, stage acting and sea life.

His personal life was no less intense. Thanks to an open marriage, his wife Agnes was busy having children with his best friend. By the time he met Marian, Lewes had given the children his name, and so he couldn't sue for divorce on grounds of adultery. Had Facebook been around then, his relationship status would have been complicated.

A Reluctant Rebel

Marian aroused Lewes's mind, as she had with so many men before him. But unlike the others, he saw past her appearance. Her best friend warned her to stay away: Lewes had a reputation. Instead, Marian ran off with him to Germany.

Back in England, she felt the sting of hypocrisy over a woman's sexuality. Lewes could come and go as before. But no one came to see her; there were no invitations to dinner. Carlyle called the two "stinkpots of humanity."

And then, out of this isolation, something extraordinary happened.

Encouraged by Lewes, she begins writing fiction—something she has always dreamed of doing. And what does she write about? Ordinary men and women. She reveals their emotional depths—she turns the mirror inside their souls—in ways that never occur to Dickens or Thackeray.

Readers at the time saw something radically new in the stories: they saw themselves. The characters were human, fallible. Like Marian Evans, they were doing their best in excruciating circumstances. "It isn't true that love makes things easy," she would later write. "It makes us choose what is difficult."

What a paradox!

Shut off by society, the writer saw that she was not alone. Marian Evans was by now profoundly aware of secrets and dangerous feelings we all keep hidden. Her own inner sexuality was completely at odds with the exterior she presented. And so, writing as George Eliot, she unlocks one of the great mysteries of human behaviour: the discrepancy between the face we present to the world and the person we are inside. Freud would study her novels for their insights.

It's easy to overlook just how radical her "experiments in writing" really were. *The Times* wrote that her characters were "so true, so natural, and so racy." The *Atheneum's* critic objected that "the brutal facts are not softened to fit them for their place in a work of Art." Eliot had mixed elements of a pastoral novel with "the startling horrors of rustic reality."

But all of these critics noted the power and skill in Eliot's realism, which ushered in the modern psychological novel. "It was really George Eliot who started it all," D.H. Lawrence would write. "It was she who started putting action inside."

*   *   *

I was 36 when I read my first George Eliot novel, and I've been hooked ever since. I fell in love with her writing, and then I began reading about her life. That is, Marian Evans' life. She was the most brilliant, fascinating woman I had ever read about.

From the biographies, I moved on to her letters. Marian was funny, even a bit snarky. Great dramatic figures tend to be at war with society, or at war with themselves. Marian Evans was at war with both.

I wanted to write a play about this passionate, complicated woman who seemed as misunderstood then as she is today.

From scandal to sympathy

Written anonymously, her first stories spoke to readers immediately. But to John Blackwood, her publisher, they were messy and unsettling, too. There was domestic abuse in the third tale, *Janet's Repentance*, and the heroine "self-medicates," as we say today. Blackwood wished the woman hadn't been driven to "so unsentimental a resource as beer."

Which brings me back to *Fleabag*.

Janet's Repentance came to mind the minute Season 2 aired, with its (ahem) attractive, "sweary" priest and his brief affair with the character played by Waller-Bridge. Talk about an unorthodox clergyman.

In Eliot's story, Janet Dempster develops feelings for her minister, Mr. Tryan. She doesn't sleep with him (there *are* some differences, after all). But the intimacy between them is real, and he confesses to sexual indiscretions in his youth. As Blackwood observed, there was indeed a transgressive nature to the stories.

And small wonder.

Marian Evans, the real George Eliot, knew from transgression. And it all began with her own scandalous life. She could never have written her stories otherwise.

When her publisher urged his new author to "soften" the stories, Marian was livid. If he saw anything "untrue to human nature," she would change it. "But alas!," she wrote, "inconsistencies and weaknesses are not untrue."

She ended the series abruptly and began *Adam Bede*. In the new novel, a young woman, Hetty Sorrel, has been seduced, impregnated, and abandoned by the squire's son. Desperate, she smothers her new-born baby. Hardly the "pretty picture" Blackwood was looking for.

Janet and Hetty are part of a long line of female characters who struggle with issues of female sexuality and powerlessness within a repressed, male-driven society. David Carroll refers to "terrible conflicts of passion and conscience" in George Eliot's novels.

Phoebe Waller-Bridge reminds us that female sexual desire continues to be problematic. As with Marian Evans, critics' unease has given way to admiration for a new kind of storytelling.

"It's just about truth and truthfulness and honesty," Waller-Bridge has said of her passion for transgressive women. I do think she enjoys giving audiences a shock or two. But her critique of women's lives, like Eliot's, is real. She's personally at daggers with the impossible standards we try living up to every day.

In *Fleabag*, Andrew Scott's priest is the only one who sees Waller-Bridge turn to the viewer—he sees that the character keeps part of herself hidden. Secret. Each time he challenges her ("Where did you just go?"), she denies it. For all the outward snark and humor, heartbreak is never far behind.

In loving Marian Evans, George Henry Lewes also saw the woman behind a mask. There was the person the world sees: someone who wants to be beautiful, charming, successful—in short, someone who falls short of society's expectations. And there was the passionate woman within: a wounded outsider, an observer in need of sympathy.

In *Janet's Repentance*, it is Mr. Tryan, the clergyman, who sees Janet's inward suffering and offers redemption. "We have all our secret sins," he tells her, "and if we knew ourselves, we should not judge each other harshly."

That sentiment, I would argue, is what Marian Evans wished to convey in all of her stories. What good is art, she wrote, if it does nothing to enlarge the sympathies?

When inner and outer worlds collide

Years ago, I sent an early draft of *A Most Dangerous Woman* to Tony-Award winning director Richard Maltby, who went on to direct the world premiere (we're now adapting the play for film). He wrote:

> What a story you have! I can't believe it's been out there and no one has ever told it. A woman married to a man she isn't married to, receiving checks addressed to a woman no one acknowledges, and world famous under an assumed name so that no one knows who she is, the center of a huge controversy she can't participate in -- she is a woman who doesn't exist. What amazing choices she made...

Imagine the reaction when Victorian England learned that George Eliot—the male cleric they assumed had written these exquisite stories—was really a woman living in sin with a married man! Marian Evans' sexual awakening had indeed led her to truths that changed the English novel forever.

We live in a world where, thanks in part to the 'Me, Too' movement, troubling truths about women's lives and vulnerability are out in the open. The novels of George Eliot seem more prescient today—more feminist—than ever before. A woman's life, she knew, was often one of thwarted ambition and desire. As a female character says in *Daniel Deronda*, "You may try -- but you can never imagine what it is to have a man's force of genius in you, and yet to suffer the slavery of being a girl."

A woman who never set out to be a rebel became the most scandalous woman in Victorian society—and began a journey into the human heart. Nearly two centuries later, her beautiful books are still leading the way.

About the Contributor

In her writing, Cathy Tempelsman is drawn to hidden figures and events from history. Her first play, A Most Dangerous Woman, was inspired by the little-known life of George Eliot. A new script, The Eleventh Hour, is based on a partisan investigation into the final day of combat during World War I. She received a commission from the New York State Council on the Arts to develop As You Loathe It, a one-act written in rhymed couplets, into a full-length play. She has also been a finalist for the Terrence McNally New Play Award and Francesca Primus Playwriting Prize, and twice nominated for the Susan Smith Blackburn Prize.

Her work has been seen in the U.S. at Barrington Stage Company, Barrow Group, Boston Playwrights Theatre, Echo Theatre, Luna Stage, New York Theater Festival, Red Bull Theater, Shakespeare Santa Cruz, Shakespeare Theatre of New Jersey, and Stageworks/Hudson.

Part 2

Her Surprising Heroines

Exceptional Women in a Prosaic Male World

Chapter 5

The Rage of the Woman Artist in George Eliot's Work

I fell in love with George Eliot aged 15, living on a remote African farm in Swaziland.

Enthralled by *Jane Eyre* earlier, I asked my father, a great novel reader, what intensely intriguing novel by another female story-teller he might suggest. He said: 'Why don't you try George Eliot? She was such a fine writer, and yet they say she had no confidence, needed reassurance, and worried that her writings were worthless'.

I drew down from the bookshelves a dusty volume of *The Mill on the Floss* (1860), with the cover illustration of a little girl, with her chin cupped in her hand as she sat and talked on the grass in a twilit scene in the open country, amongst some strange-looking (Gypsy) folk in still stranger garb. They were cooking on an open fire, surrounded by caravans.

Paging through, I discovered that the girl, Maggie Tulliver, had run away from home, where she'd felt unappreciated, to join the brown-skinned Gypsies who, she felt, looked just like her - only to be returned, later, to her father.

I thus encountered a writer who had a special empathy for individuals who felt they didn't quite 'fit in'; who pitied peoples like Gypsies and Jews, who were often outcasts in their adopted countries; but, always complex, she explored negative possibilities for host countries too, notably in *Daniel Deronda* and her poetry.

She exposed the grim existence meted out at times to 'eccentric' artists, not least if they were women and had a contribution to make. Even leading thinkers thought females only fit for rearing children; and they were sometimes regarded as tainted, 'unsexed', if they entered such 'men's professions' as writing.

Eliot often counteracts such fallacies in the action of her stories, but she seems to some extent to have also internalised stereotypes, describing herself, and also Maggie (with some irony), as 'a mistake of nature' (Book l, Chapter. 2; cf *L*, ll, 160).

Turning to the beginning of this lovely book, I was enchanted by this new, wise-seeming writer, whose very emotional little protagonist seemed modelled on herself – though I knew nothing else about the author: sometimes an advantage.

I quickly became passionately engaged with the story, with its intelligent heroine whose adventures - where things often don't turn out well for her – grabbed my heart-strings. Maggie has the temperament of a frustrated artist; and touchingly, she almost, as a post-adolescent, lonely girl, has a love affair with a hunchbacked young man who was attracted to her when both were children; but her rather brutal brother, Tom, intercedes.

Philip is an able artist, and his crooked back, like Maggie's brown skin, marks them both as vulnerable outsiders. Characters in Eliot's *oeuvre* who have what Latimer, the narrator of her novella, 'The Lifted Veil' (1859), describes as 'the artist's sensibility without his voice', often end up frustrated, even tragically so, as do Maggie and Philip.

As a realist writer, Eliot most commonly demonstrates the exasperating disruption of female ambition, rather than success which misleadingly underestimates difficulty. In Book IV, Chapter. 3 of *The Mill*, Maggie resents the 'feeble' girl's education which she has had to accept as her due, based on her gender.

Eliot is at her most powerful depicting the slow, poisonous growth of anger that culminates in homicidal rage, in women who are seriously oppressed at home, or by their husbands, as indeed they were only too often in a patriarchal society. She demonstrates clearly that girls have strong, driven emotions - a will of their own despite attempts to corset their lives according to over-rationalised stereotypes. Maggie, more intelligent than anyone in her family, reaches a point where she realises that, as a girl, she has been deprived of 'part of her inherited share in the hard-won treasures of thought' – a social suppression shown to be potentially dangerous: perhaps an issue for the novelist herself:

> [S]he fainted under her loneliness, and fits even of anger and hatred towards her father and mother, who were so unlike what she would have them be..., would flow out over her affections and conscience like a lava stream, and frighten her with a sense that it was not difficult for her to become a demon (Book IV, Chapter. 3).

Maggie virtually absconds with her cousin Lucy's admirer ultimately, but with remorse and generosity returns home, to be vilified in her neighbourhood as an unmarried and therefore a 'fallen' woman.

Some Victorian readers thought Maggie wicked; girls were forbidden to read the later parts of the book; a young woman caught with it was reprimanded from the pulpit. June Skye Szirotny pertinently points out that this novel, illustrating as it does Maggie's ultimate defeat, is historically important because 'there are few stories of girls' suffering under patriarchy... [T]ragedies of adolescent girls, such as Maggie, were hidden in the hedgerows.'[1] Maggie's childhood reading about 'ducked' witches who were drowned, and thus proved innocent, reaches its fulfilment at her tragic end.

Young Islamic girls doing English literature courses have said how easily they identify with Maggie. Eliot and her unforgettable heroine have passionately inspired later, celebrated women, such as Emily Dickinson and Vera Brittain, who've seen her as their role model.

Gifted Caterina in Eliot's novella, 'Mr Gilfil's Love Story',[2] an adopted Italian girl and an accomplished operatic performer, finds that her drawing-room singing and harp-playing relieve her grieving anger at being exploited sexually by a young man from a higher class.

The extent of this misuse remains unclear. Though the pair meet secretly in the woods and exchange locks of hair, he elects to marry a woman of his own social status, to which Caterina does not belong. Eliot tells us: 'And her singing...lost none of its energy...[It] seemed to be lifting the pain from her heart...' (Chapter.10).

---

[1] June Skye Szirotny, *George Eliot's Feminism; 'The Right to Rebellion'* (Basingstoke, 2015), p229, n 73.

[2] In *Scenes of Clerical Life* (1857).

She is the plaything of Captain Wybrow, whom she loves unrequitedly. Her art liberates her, albeit temporarily: 'All the passion that made her misery was hurled by a convulsive effort into her music' (Chapter. 13); 'she ceased to be passive, and became prominent'.

Art alone gives women status: 'She herself sometimes wondered how it was that, whether she felt sad or angry..., it was always a relief to her to sing. Those full deep notes she sent forth seemed to be...carrying away the madness of her brain' (Chapter 10).

Art is treated by Eliot as cathartic, preventing extreme pathological states especially in women whose energies are thwarted, even violently, by social convention. Caterina is also traumatised by her condescending English family's attempts to 'train this little papist into a good Protestant, and graft as much English fruit as possible on the Italian stem' (Chapter. 3). She ultimately seizes a dagger – a melodramatic *leitmotif* with Eliot's female performers - and attempts to stab the young captain, only to find him dead from heart failure when she reaches their meeting-place at the rookery.

Such passages counteract the current, not uncommon 19th-century view that girls should only be 'permitted to think under supervision', since woman is 'nothing, of herself'; her very 'smiles and tears are not exclusively her own', but the property of her husband and father. So wrote the author of a popular handbook.[3]

In this story calamity results from the head of this upper-class family's paternalistic despotism – from Sir

---

[3]Mrs [Sara] Ellis, *The Daughters of England, Their Position in Society, Character, & Responsibilities* (London, 1842). Popular in its day, this reactionary book has become notorious.

Christopher's attempts to enforce marriages of his own choosing, including Tina's. This leaves two people dead and the others, including the penitent despot, miserable.

Pericles, the ancient Athenian president, had said that for a woman to put herself on display publicly was 'detestable', an idea which reverberated through the ages particularly in a society like 19th-century Britain, which saw itself as the spiritual inheritor of Classical Culture.

This taboo, internalised by girls, was often difficult to navigate emotionally. But for Caterina, while 'her fingers were wandering with their old sweet method among the keys,...her soul was floating in its true familiar element of delicious sound, as the water plant that lies withered and shrunken on the ground expands into freedom and beauty when once more bathed in its native flood' (Ch. 20).

Another celebrated singer, the eponymous heroine of the verse drama, 'Armgart', claims that her art has saved her from homicidal impulses (unlike Laure in *Middlemarch*, who actually murders her husband onstage with a real dagger) in a much-quoted passage:

> 'Poor wretch!' she says, of any murderess -
> 'The world was cruel, and she could not sing:
>
> I carry my revenges in my throat;
> I love in singing, and am loved again.'

As one critic has commented about such passages, women deprived of an outlet such as the artist enjoys can 'give vent to anger depraved by impotence'[4] Armgart contemptuously refuses an aristocrat's

---

[4]Gillian Beer, *George Eliot* (Brighton, 1986).

proposal of marriage with the proviso that she give up her career, a sacrifice he prizes for himself; but tragically she loses her voice, which demotes her to the common lot of women.

Daniel Deronda (1876), a dark yet luminous work, is my favourite Eliot novel after *The Mill,* partly because it truthfully depicts 19th-century artists' everyday lives as disturbing and difficult. It is also the most powerful depiction in Eliot's writing of sustained, murderous female rage resulting from sadistic male power, causing temporary psychic implosion.

The young heroine, the complex, astonishing Gwendolen Harleth, has ambitions to perform, but has insufficient talent outside mediocre drawing rooms, enforcing her resort to marriage to a sadistic man, named Grandcourt by the narrator – an appalling mockery - because her family have lost their fortunes through the gambling of an unscrupulous finance company. Another artist, the 'Jewess' Mirah Lapidoth, performs ably and is a sought-after singer, once she's established in aristocratic London homes. A third, Alcharisi, is a retired, distinguished world-famous opera singer, also of Jewish origin. Eliot portrays a male artist of genius, too: Herr Klesmer. *He* is a mentor to several women artists in the novel - a Liszt or a Rubenstein and a hybrid of German, Jew and Slav, who explicates his credo of artistic dedication to Gwendolen (who seeks his advice). Dedication he regards as a prerequisite of great art. He comments on the hard lot of women onstage, including potential sexual abuse. But:

> I am not decrying the life of the true artist. I am exalting it. I say, it is out of the reach of any but choice organisations – natures framed to love perfection and to labour for

it...But the honour comes from the inward vocation and the hard-won achievement (Chapter. 23).[5]

Klesmer insists bleakly to Gwendolen, an aspiring actress, that she must 'subdue her mind to unbroken discipline.' Initially, genius is 'little more than a great capacity for receiving discipline...Your muscles – your whole frame – must go like a watch, true, true, true, to a hair. That is the work of springtime, before habits have been determined.' She must learn to bear herself 'on the stage, as a horse, however beautiful, must be trained for the circus' (ibid). Art is a calling, not a means simply to earning money.

There is much satire against philistines who view the artist as a commodity. Possessing a 'world-wide celebrity' would 'make [an artist] great to the most ordinary people because of their knowledge of his great expensiveness.' (Chapter. 10). Mrs Arrowpoint views Klesmer as 'a man who has been paid to come to the house – who is nobody knows what – a Gypsy, a Jew, a mere bubble of the earth' (Chapter. 22).

Another philistine is Mr Bult, 'a political platitudinarian as insensible as an ox to everything he can't turn into political capital', according to Klesmer.

When Klesmer makes a striking political point at dinner, Bult responds, 'With all my heart....I knew he had too much talent to be a mere musician.' Klesmer fires up:

---

[5]For an account of how Klesmer's speeches seem partly framed to counteract Wagner's anti-Semitic rantings in *Judaism in Music* (1869), see my *George Eliot and Victorian Attitudes to Racial Diversity* (Lampeter, 2003), pp 506-24.

'Ah, sir, you are under some mistake there...Nobody has too much talent to be a mere musician. Most men have too little. A creative artist is no more a mere musician than a great statesman is a mere politician. We are not ingenious puppets, sir, who live in a box and look out on the world only when it is gaping for amusement.'

The unique aristocratic caste to which Klesmer (and Eliot, clearly) elevate the artist is no idle boast. 'We count ourselves on level benches with legislators' (Ch. 22).

Mirah Lapidoth, a type of 'Wandering Jew' who early on performs everywhere from Budapest and Germany to New York, draws attention to the actress's hazardous life, including sexual misuse. In Vienna, she says, 'I was miserable...Men came about us and wanted to talk to me: women and men seemed to look at me with a sneering smile...,[ ] the people strutting, quarrelling, leering – the faces with cunning and malice in them...I had seen what despised women were' (Chapter. 20).

Even her unscrupulous father treats Mirah as an object: 'I saw that his wishing me to sing the greatest music, and parts in grand operas, was only wishing for what would fetch the greatest price' (Chapter. 20). He has pushed her hard into her profession, damaging her voice. For a while she had to sing in seedy music halls. She escaped when her father had attempted to sell her into prostitution and had left her alone in a room with a disreputable Count near a music-hall of dubious repute.

These complex pictures are rounded off with the hero Daniel Deronda's remarkable, lost and later found

Jewish mother, Alcharisi or the Princess, the brilliant singer and rebel who repudiated her patriarchal father; she has also rejected the stereotype of all women as loving mothers. She gave up her very young son to her English, upper-class admirer, Sir Hugo Mallinger; and she tells Daniel: '...I ought to say I felt about you as other women say they feel about their children. I did *not* feel that. I was glad to be freed from you' (Ch. 51).

Alcharisi was prepared to sacrifice much to be an artist, to experience 'a myriad lives in one' and eschew Jewish particularism. 'I delivered you from the pelting contempt that pursues Jewish separateness'; 'I was not like a brute, obliged to go with my own herd'; 'I rid myself of the Jewish tatters and gibberish'. 'I cared for the wide world and all I could represent in it', says the Princess, though her powerful ego requires that she be its medium.

With vitriolic passion she repudiates the arbitrary imposition of narrow gender roles, uttering the famous words: 'You may try, but you can never imagine what it is to have a man's force of genius in you, and yet to suffer the slavery of being a girl'. For the Princess, patriarchy is death:

> 'To have a pattern cut out - "this is the Jewish woman; this is what she must be;...a woman's heart must be of such size and no larger, else it must be pressed small, like Chinese feet; her happiness is to be made as cakes are, by a fixed receipt." That was what my father wanted (Chapter. 51).

Yet years later the Princess, despite her own opposition, is compelled by obscure, subconscious psychic forces to yield to her father's will, since she is dying from a painful disease. The tremendous strain of her sustained repudiation of her father, possibly the cause of her illness, has not after all been sufficient to resist institutionalised male dominance, which has had a determining power over generations in gender relations, over aeons – and it is this that, no doubt, accounts for George Eliot's depiction of the tremendous difficulties ambitious women face in their careers.

Alcharisi feels that she had a right to obey the promptings of her own genius: '[A]cknowledge that I had a right to be an artist, though my father's will was against it. My nature gave me a charter' (Chapter. 51).

Altogether, Eliot's views on women artists were complex, though she had little patience with amateurs or writers of 'silly novels'. The double binds she employs reveal her bleak scepticism: talented women deprived of education, or the ability to be creative, suffer, but there are likely pitfalls, also, awaiting those who are more fortunate.

Some writers of the 1980s claimed that Eliot was 'no feminist', but surely her powerful tragedies, that show women who are deeply wounded or pathologised by a suppressing patriarchal society, which Charisi views as death oriented, create an *edge* of protest. Laure becomes a murderess for reasons not given. Gwendolen, a victim of terrible abuse with no true artistic or cultural outlet, is instrumental in her brutal husband Grandcourt's death; and yet she is redeemed. No one is sorry when Grandcourt drowns after he has fallen overboard from his yacht, and Gwendolen hesitates to throw him the rope he cries for: 'I saw him sink... "The rope!" he called out... - and I held my hand, and my heart said, "Die!" – and he sank...'

Klesmer insists on selfless dedication to produce great art, and this suggests that ultimately, the artist is the medium or incubator of art, and her ego associated with it is of negligible importance. Ironically, Deronda probably perpetuates a patriarchal society when he ventures to the East in search of a place for Jewish people to settle, while his now wife, Mirah, clearly gives up her singing career.

Eliot's passionate, uniquely complicated view of life makes her my favourite of novelists.

About the Contributor

Brenda McKay grew up in Swaziland and South Africa. Her undergraduate degree was secured at the University of Witwatersrand in Johannesburg, South Africa. She earned an M.A. in Victorian Studies (cum laude) and a Ph.D in Victorian Literature and Science, both at Birkbeck College, University of London.

She has taught at Wits University in South Africa, at Birkbeck College, London, and Hertfordshire University.

She has written widely on Victorian Culture and Science. Her monograph, *George Eliot and Victorian Attitudes to Racial Diversity* (2003) was honoured by CHOICE as an outstanding academic work of the year. She reviews new books regularly for The George Eliot Review.

Chapter 6

"The secrets of sorrow:" Uncovering Mental Illness in *Janet's Repentance*

Katharine Williams

The first time I opened George Eliot's *Janet's Repentance*, I was curled up in a window seat overlooking the Blue Ridge Mountains. It was fall break of my senior year of college, and I had taken a trip with a few close friends to North Carolina. After an unrelenting season of pain and loss, the trip was an eagerly anticipated breath of fresh air. After losing my grandfather, enduring the end of a difficult relationship, and dealing with a succession of traumatic family emergencies, I felt I barely had the time to process my emotions.

Three thousand feet above sea level, nestled in the quiet of the mountains, I was hoping for some respite. What I didn't expect to encounter was the comfort and hope offered by a paperback I borrowed from my English professor.

Janet's Repentance is one of Eliot's lesser-known works (I had certainly never heard of it before my professor lent me her copy). However, it's inconspicuous status in comparison to *Middlemarch* or *Daniel Deronda* makes it a no less powerful read.

It is quite possibly the first descriptive portrait of a middle-class female alcoholic in nineteenth-century fiction. Serialized anonymously in *Blackwood's Magazine* between January and November of 1857, and later published as part of *Scenes of Clerical Life* in 1858, the novella tells the story of Janet Dempster, an alcoholic abused by her husband, who finds redemption through her relationship with the Reverend Tryan.

Janet's Repentance is also a story that sheds light on "the secrets of sorrow" and haunting visions we recognize today as depression and trauma (Eliot 350).

Countering the Victorian tendency to find fault in the person who is suffering, Eliot instead offers a picture of these mental conditions that elicits both respect and sympathy, through her characterization of Janet. Indeed, Eliot's depiction of an abused, traumatized, depressed woman is harrowing – even her publisher, John Blackwood, suggested the author paint "a pleasanter picture" for her reader (Letters 2: 244). However, it is this raw portrait of Janet, who possesses an enduring, dignified strength, that deeply touched me as I read the novella from my window seat. It is this story which contributed to my own healing.

It is first important to talk about how Eliot portrays Janet's abuse. The author does not shy away from depicting the horrific violence of Janet's mistreatment, starting with the couple's first real interaction of the novella.

After an evening of leading demonstrations against the new evangelical minister, the Reverend Tryan, Janet's husband returns home furiously intoxicated. Robert Dempster quickly turns on his wife as he walks through the door, accusing her of drinking, laying "his hand with a firm grip on her shoulder," and striking her again and again (Eliot 285).

This physical abuse only worsens as the novella progresses. In the scene of perhaps the greatest brutality, Dempster drunkenly marches up the stairs and forces Janet from their bed. Standing trembling and "helpless in her night-dress before her husband," Janet appears powerless in the face of his cruelty (Eliot 342). Her husband throws her out of their home, and into the frozen, blustering March night.

It is this violence that leaves Janet not only physically bruised, but profoundly mentally scarred. "Crushed with anguish and despair," she experiences intense feelings of depression, distressing nightmares, and disturbing visions of her husband returning to attack her, after she takes refuge with her neighbour Mrs. Pettifer (Eliot 343). Consider Janet's vision in the following passage, one we would now recognize as indicative of trauma:

> But her imagination influenced by physical depression as well as by mental habits, was haunted by the vision of her husband's return home, and she began to shudder with the yesterday's dread. She heard him calling her, she saw him going to her mother's to look for her, she felt sure he would find her out, and burst in upon her.
> (Eliot 372)

Here, as Janet is overwhelmed by the memory of her husband's abuse, her body seems to relive the attack. She *shudders* with dread, just as she *trembled* the night she was thrown out of her home. She also imaginatively hears and sees her husband, as if her senses are poised for another attack.

As Jill Matus discusses, "...well before Freud, Victorian conceptions of consciousness were already capable of supporting a theory of mental injury in which powerful emotion could produce trance-like effects, disrupt memory, and disturb affect regulation" (Matus). Here, Janet's corporeal response and disturbed imagination perhaps speak to these early theories of "mental injury."

It is also interesting that Eliot frequently links Janet's mental state to her physical being. For example, when Janet wakes after her first night in Mrs. Pettifer's home, the narrator describes her life of "fevered despair" (Eliot 348). "Fevered" implies a nervous agitation, but also links her desperation to disease. As Janet reflects on her situation, and wrestles with whether or not to seek counsel from the Reverend Tryan, she then feels a "leaden weight of discouragement" pressing upon her "more and more heavily" (Eliot 351). She is rendered almost physically paralyzed as she experiences "a motionless vacant misery" (Eliot 352). In the midst of her depression, Janet barely has the strength to lean her "aching head on her hands" (Eliot 352).

Eliot's heroine feels crushed, sickened and immobilized, as she experiences the weight of her grief and hopelessness. For those of us who know someone suffering from depression, or who suffer ourselves, this description of Janet's pain certainly strikes a chord.

Why might Eliot portray Janet's affliction in these terms?

Much like the scientific thinkers of her time, Eliot believed that the "mind and body are mutually bound up" (Davis 11). Since "British psychiatry evinced a somatic bias throughout the nineteenth century," this emphasis on the inseparable relationship between mind and body likely influenced her depiction of her suffering heroine (Oppenheim 36).

Eliot's portrayal of Janet's mental state perhaps also counters traditional Victorian attitudes towards "melancholia" and "shock" – terms used to describe what we would now classify as depression and trauma (Hill and Deborde 6). While there was movement to treat mental disorders more humanely in the nineteenth century – the term "mad doctor" was becoming outdated by the 1840s – limited psychological understanding resulted in a strong stigma surrounding mental illness (Oppenheim 27).

As Jill Matus discusses in her exploration of trauma in nineteenth-century British literature, Victorian culture tended to be one of blame. While nineteenth-century authors may have depicted fictional protagonists responding to a traumatic event, it is likely that those characters did "...something to render them guilty and divided" (Matus).

Indeed, mental illness was interpreted by some as a punishment for sin and thus "worthy of censure" (Oppenheim 49). Those suffering were often deemed "useless to society" or a threat to their families (Oppenheim 49). Even those who treated mental disorders were considered lower on the totem pole of professional medicine (Oppenheim 40).

In light of this cultural attitude, what might Eliot's readers have made of the visceral depiction of Janet's suffering?

It is important to note that in the context of the novella, Janet is mentally suffering as a victim of abuse – one who has turned to alcohol as a crutch. In an age when wives were frequently blamed for their spouse's behaviour, and the female alcoholic was regarded as a "particularly villainous type of fallen woman," Eliot's reader may not have been immediately sympathetic with Janet's plight (Hammerton 47, and Skelly 5).

However, as Eliot wrote in *A Natural History of German Life*, an essay published one year before she began work on *Scenes of Clerical Life*, art's primary purpose is "the extension of our sympathies" (Eliot, *A Natural History of German Life*). Indeed, the mind and body relationship she uses while depicting Janet's mental state may in fact serve this purpose, extending sensitivity and compassion. By linking Janet's hopelessness and despair to physical experiences of pain, Eliot perhaps further validates her protagonist's suffering. Janet's internal affliction following her abuse is equally as onerous and just as real as a physical illness or paralysis. Her suffering must be considered with genuine compassion, for it is serious and authentic.

It is essential to also think about Eliot's depiction of Janet's physical and emotional suffering, alongside the rather regal, Christ-like description of her heroine. When the narrator describes the first abusive encounter between Janet and her husband, he simultaneously imagines Janet's mother praying and weeping for her daughter. He notes a picture drawn by Janet, which hangs over her mother's mantelpiece: "She too has a picture over her mantelpiece, drawn in chalk by Janet long years ago. She looked at it before she went to bed. It is a head bowed beneath a cross, and wearing a crown of thorns" (Eliot 285). Given this picture is Janet's artwork, and her mother is imagining her daughter's plight, the painting may suggest Janet's divine characteristics. Like Christ wearing a crown of thorns, she is a faithful innocent subjected to unjust violence.

The narrator also describes Janet, from her mother's perspective, as a "tall white arum" (Eliot 285). White again connotes a sense of blamelessness, while biblically, the arum lily is a symbol of Christ.

This divine portrayal of Janet continues even as she endures the mental ramifications of her abuse. When she arrives at Mrs. Pettifer's she is described as a "tall white figure" (Eliot 343). Janet's neighbour then kindly wraps her in as much drapery as she can find for someone so tall, to keep her warm after a fitful nightmare (Eliot 351). Here, Janet appears as a robed woman of stature, gracefully regal and perhaps even angelic, in the midst of her depression and trauma. Indeed, the narrator continues to emphasize her "tall graceful unconstrained figure" throughout the novella (Eliot 288). This language highlights Janet's beauty and perhaps further suggests her power, as she is physically elevated above the rest of her community due to her height.

Notably, Janet is not perfect. The novella's title suggests as much, as she comes to repent of her sins to the Reverend Tryan, who helps to renew her faith and restore her hope. Yet, Eliot continues to attribute a sort of divine strength to Janet in spite of her imperfections and throughout her intense depressive and traumatic episodes.

Through this characterisation, Eliot elicits both sympathy and respect for her protagonist. Janet is an innocent victim of abuse. She is battling mental illness. And she is a woman of strength – an empowering combination for a Victorian reader as well as a twenty-first century one.

Indeed, for me that fall break, encountering Eliot's heroine deepened my compassion for others and for myself. As I sympathized with Janet from my window seat, I recognized my closest friend's experience of abuse, my sister's struggle with mental illness, and my own experience of trauma and depression.

To be touched by Janet's pain was to acutely feel my own, and to share in the suffering of the women I hold dear. Eliot reminded me that this pain deserves recognition and the utmost compassion. I also acknowledged my own strength in the midst of struggle. I am only five feet, three inches (and a half), but I also have Janet's stature, or her strength, power and endurance – as do my friends, family members and so many others who are living with mental health conditions.

It is this lived and shared experience that can contribute to transformation.

Janet encounters healing when she asks to see the Reverend Tryan, who she believes has known "the secrets of sorrow" (Eliot 350). The Reverend then chooses to share his painful history with her, when his "mind was dark" (Eliot 360):

> And Janet's anguish was not strange to Mr. Tryan. He had never been in the presence of a sorrow and a self-despair that had sent so strong a thrill through all the recesses of his saddest experience; and it is because sympathy is but a living again through our own past in a new form.
> (Eliot 358)

By recognising their shared pain and choosing to voice his experience, Mr. Tryan consequently catalyses Janet's healing. Thus, Eliot illustrates the power of recognizing our common experiences of suffering. Seeing our own history in another helps to bring hope and change.

For me, this fresh revelation prompted a new season of restoration, one where I felt empowered to lean on those around me, to speak honestly about my mental health, and to see the value of my experiences, while acknowledging my pain.

I am grateful to Eliot for extending my sympathy, for helping me to appreciate my strength, and for giving "new form" to my own secret sorrows.

Bibliography

Davis, Michael. George Eliot and Nineteenth-century Psychology: Exploring the Unmapped Territory. Ashgate Publishing, 2006.

DeBorde, Alisa M., "Seeing Trauma: The Known and the Hidden in Nineteenth-Century Literature." 2018. Graduate Theses and Dissertations. http://scholarcommons.usf.edu/etd/7141.

Eliot, George The George Eliot Letters. 9 vols. Ed. Gordon S. Haight. New Haven: Yale UP, 1955-1978.

"Janet's Repentance." Scenes of Clerical Life. Penguin Books, 1973.

"The Natural History of German Life," George Eliot Archive, http://georgeeliotarchive.org/items/show/100.

Hammerton, A. James. Cruelty and Companionship: Conflict in Nineteenth-Century Married Life. Routledge, 1992.

Hill, Simon A, and Richard Laugharne. "Mania, dementia and melancholia in the 1870s: admissions to a Cornwall asylum." Journal of the Royal Society of Medicine vol. 96, no. 7 (2003): 361-3.

Matus, Jill L. "Psychological trauma Victorian style: from perpetrators to victims." The Lancet, Vol. 376, no. 9739, August 2010, 410- 411.

Oppenheim, Janet. "Shattered Nerves": Doctors, Patients, and Depression in Victorian England. Oxford University Press, 1991.

Skelly, Julia. "When Seeing is Believing: Women, Alcohol and Photography in Victorian

Britain." Shift: Queen's Journal of Visual and Material Culture, vol.1, 2008, 1-17.

About the Author

Katharine Williams recently graduated from the College of William & Mary in Williamsburg, Virginia where she double majored in English Literature and French.

Her English honors thesis focused on the role of hands in George Eliot's early fiction. As a William & Mary Honors Fellow, she received funding to study at the British Library and Wellcome Library for this project. Drawing on this research, Katharine presented at the George Eliot 2019 Bicentenary Conference in Leicester this July.

After spending a year teaching English in Annecy, France, Katharine hopes to continue exploring her fascination with nineteenth-century British literature and George Eliot in graduate school.

Chapter 7

. *The Mill on the Floss* –
A Spiritual Autobiography

Mari Seaword

'My books are deeply serious things to me, and come out of all the painful discipline, all the most hardly-learnt lessons of my past life.' (*The George Eliot Letters*, iii, 187)

George Eliot's *The Mill on the Floss* is the story of a young girl's journey to maturity. The heroine Maggie Tulliver's journey reflects the journey of the writer Marian Evans (George Eliot) herself.

The novel has a great deal of the personal feelings of the author and that makes this work compelling. It expresses her innermost concerns and the sublimation of private agony that she herself went through. This dynamic is the irresistible force of this novel.

George Eliot wrote this masterpiece by wielding her pen with great emotion. Now where do we find the source of that strong emotion?

When we look at the life of Marian Evans, we find two kinds of anguish caused by the disparity between her beliefs and social conventions.

One is about her Christian faith, and the other is about her attitudes to marriage. When she abandoned her faith in God and refused to go to church, that disquieted her father. When she met George Henry Lewes and determined to live together as man and wife, her beloved brother Isaac disowned her.

This rift between Marian and her brother was a recurring source of distress to her and she wrote *The Mill on the Floss* during such a distressing period. Because she herself suffered anguish about the external demands of duty and the internal needs of love, she was able to embody the internal conflicts between duty and love in Maggie Tulliver.

Characteristics of Love

In *The Mill on the Floss*, Maggie has a very different personality from that of her beloved brother Tom. He is 'one of those lads that grow everywhere in England' (from the novel, Book I, Chapter 5) whereas she is strongly individual both in appearance and in mind. She is a bright girl yet shows her emotions so openly and behaves as a child of nature.

Victorians were inclined to sanctify the innocence of childhood but Maggie is not an angel of a girl, pure and beautiful. The scene in the attic effectively shows Maggie's character. We find the scene funny as Maggie's behaviour is effervescent and piquant and entirely free from the constraints that grown-ups have.

Maggie's single-minded love for her brother Tom is glimpsed on almost every page of the first volume. Although Maggie is volatile and feels joys and sorrows for trivial things in her daily life, the most powerful ruler of her emotions is Tom. He has a decisive influence on her sensitive feelings. The characteristic of Maggie's love can be observed through her relationship with her brother.

Maggie loves her brother more than anyone else and she ungrudgingly pours out the whole of her affection on Tom. However, Maggie's love is not a divine love. She always desires her love to be rewarded by being loved in return. She expresses her affection simply because she wants to be loved. 'The need of being loved' is 'the strongest need in poor Maggie's nature.' (Book I, Chapter 5)

Maggie's love is earnest and deep but her great happiness exists in the reward itself. When love is reciprocated, it brings perfect union between two people but the joy of the union never arises otherwise. Wishing to be loved, Maggie loves others so ardently. This theme of love and the need of being loved are of great significance throughout Marian Evans's life as well.

From Self-Awareness to Renunciation

'The golden gate' of Maggie's childhood had for ever closed behind her and Maggie becomes conscious of her *self* as she entered 'the thorny wilderness' (Book II, Chapter 7) with the coming of her adolescence.

The customs of her community that are based on traditionally fixed ideas gradually begin to strike her as incompatible with her own convictions. This incompatibility makes her rebellious and she experiences difficulties in coming to terms with social conventions.

These characteristics overlap in many ways with those of the author in her youth. Here we find the disparity between the generations that brings pain and difficulties to Maggie. It reveals the process of Maggie's initial renunciation of her personal values, in which the author described the collision between individual and community.

The influential ideas in the community are represented by the Dodsons and the Tullivers. 'The religion of the Dodsons consisted in revering whatever was customary and respectable' (Book IV, Chapter 1). It seems that their unenlightened ideas are easily seated in traditional customs. Their religion is merely in name and it cannot be the salvation of a suffering soul.

They are living in an age that swallows anything from the past and a carefree life exists in ignorance rather than in learning. These are the conditions that cause pain to Maggie and oppress her. She cannot put confidence in conventional religion or material prosperity.

Under these circumstances, it is inevitable that a girl like Maggie becomes aware of her *self*. Maggie cannot easily follow such conventions but at the same time she cannot sever her relations with the surroundings she was brought up in. Two contrary feelings coming from a rebellious spirit against the middle-class narrowness, and from a fateful sense of solidarity with the customs of the community, arise in Maggie, and there she stands in a dilemma.

The theme of tragic conflicts between generations is unfolded here. A person of high integrity is bound to face such conflicts.

Maggie's soul is always craving for something sublime, and 'some volcanic upheavings of imprisoned passions' (Book IV, Chapter 3) appear in her face at intervals. However, she experiences nothing but frustration as she earnestly thirsts for a high moral, aesthetic and intellectual value.

In consequence, she discovers peace in self-renunciation and renunciation is the only way to salvation for Maggie, who stands in a dilemma. She can come to terms with the customs of renunciation only because she wishes, more than anything else, to be loved by Tom, who is a symbol of the conventional world.

Maggie's strong ties to her brother are fateful. While Tom grows up to be the kind of person the world approves of, that is dutiful and proud, Maggie becomes the kind of person the world judges harshly.

A woman ahead of her time, brimming with intelligence and imagination, Maggie becomes increasingly difficult for her brother and the rest of her family to understand. She has to live in confrontation with the conventional community.

Through Maggie's process of renunciation, we find conflicts between generations. As Rosemary Ashton observes in *George Eliot* (1983), Eliot's essays in 1855 and 1856 prove that she applied philosophical principles to literature. The term that she used in those essays was 'evolution'. In *The Mill on the Floss*, we can see one aspect of her ideas on 'evolution' in the plot that the new generation is destined to experience conflict with older customs in order to make progress.

Conflicts between Duty and Love

Although Maggie regards renunciation as the best virtue, her belief in self-renunciation is swayed by Philip Wakem. When we try to understand how Philip's existence has influenced Maggie, we should remind ourselves of Maggie's nature. Maggie has wanted to be loved since she was a girl, and she fully expresses her love towards Tom simply because she wanted him to love her. However, Tom is insusceptible to her delicate feelings and doesn't reward Maggie for her affection. In comparison with Tom, Philip has cherished and hinted at a deep affection for Maggie and has cared about her feelings.

Maggie also has an acute wish to become well educated and Philip is someone who can quench her thirst for learning.

While the customs of their community are a cage for Maggie, Philip tries to release her from them. Philip is the only dependable ally for Maggie and he is the only one who can appease her thirst for beauty and learning. Maggie's natural desire to display her ability emerges in her friendship with Philip, who has a sensitive heart and an artistic temperament.

Maggie has been inclined to express sympathy for unfortunate people since her girlhood. When Philip asks Maggie to see him, it is very hard for Maggie to refuse as she thinks it will be a kindness to him and 'an opportunity indicated for making her mind more worthy of its highest service.' (Book V, Chapter 3) Besides, she has always longed to be loved and Philip is 'the only person who has ever seemed to love her devotedly.' (Book VI, Chapter 2)

They are very exceptional in their community and they have no one but each other to satisfy their demands.

Maggie has already felt an inward conflict because her assignation with Philip is a treasonable act against her father and brother under the circumstances, namely the strife between the Tullivers and the Wakems over the mill. Maggie is in constant fear that their secret may be discovered.

As she is bound by loyalty to her father and brother, she is not entirely happy during the secret meeting. It is obvious that she feels the conflict between duty and love. Duty binds Maggie to loyalty to father and brother while love brings gratification and liberation to her.

The conflicts between duty and love are the nucleus of this tragedy; the pitiable scenes between Maggie and Philip are an omen of her future relationship with Stephen. The agitation gradually adds to Maggie's grief as the realities of her surroundings are revealed.

The pangs of love pervade the major novels of George Eliot and that seems to be their greatest theme. It appears that the root of the theme is the personal agony that the author herself experienced.

We can well imagine that the author ruminated over the decision that she made at the age of thirty-four by depicting her heroines in emotional angst. Although the situation of each heroine is different from the real life of Marian Evans, the plot that the heroines experience, the inward conflicts between duty and love, is the same as her own experiences.

In fact, she was leading an uneasy life while she was writing this very novel because she was forsaken by her beloved brother Isaac due to her liaison with G. H. Lewes.

She took marriage seriously and regarded her own irregular but deeply fulfilling relationship with Lewes as if it were a marriage properly solemnised by the Church and recognised in law.[1] Her *marriage* with Lewes was illicit and against the Victorian moral sense,

---

[1] *Oxford Reader's Companion to George Eliot*, ed. John Rignall, Oxford University Press, 2000, p.250.

but that was the ideal relationship for which she had longed.

Both the heroine Maggie and the author Marian experienced the inward conflicts between duty and love. One chose duty, while the other chose love; but the important thing here is not the result but the process.

Humanity over Animality

Ever since Maggie met her cousin Lucy's fiancé Stephen, Maggie and Stephen feel irresistible attraction for each other and their love is declared in spite of themselves.

Love between Maggie and Stephen here is totally different from the spiritual love between Maggie and Philip. The story reaches the climax here and the current of the story vehemently changes into a torrent.

Maggie has already experienced a dilemma between duty and love but Stephen's love for Maggie appears to engulf everything that she has cherished such as faith, conscience, and duty. Stephen draws Maggie to himself so abruptly and easily and the driving force that unites the two seems to be rather violent.

What on earth is it?

The lack of description about Stephen makes it seem implausible that Maggie so easily falls in love with Stephen and betrays both Philip and her dear cousin Lucy. We are left bewildered there.

However, if we go back to the text again, we realise that the driving force that unites Maggie and Stephen originates in sexuality. Treating love as a sensual experience was hardly acceptable to the Victorian moral sense and it was rather an offence against Victorian standards.

Although humans are notoriously fallible and we all experience sexual temptation, what is the message that George Eliot wanted to convey?

In her reply to Sir Edward Bulwer-Lytton, who criticized the tryst scenes between Maggie and Stephen, she explained: 'The other chief point of criticism – Maggie's position towards Stephen – is too vital a part of my whole conception and purpose for me to be converted to the condemnation of it. If I am wrong there – if I did not really know what my heroine would feel and do under the circumstances in which I deliberately placed her, I ought not to have written this book at all, but quite a different book, if any.' (*The George Eliot Letters*, iii, 317-18) The affair between Maggie and Stephen contains the message that George Eliot really wanted to convey.

One way of interpreting this message could be that she wished to stress the fact that humans have a spiritual existence beyond the merely animal. Although we certainly see that the relationship between Maggie and Stephen is based on their sexual feelings, the moral senses or human virtues gradually stand out in clear relief against animality.

The author consistently describes the inner conflicts between desires and duty, or conscience, or human ties. Her description of sexuality must be nothing but an element to balance against spirituality.

The scenes where Maggie is torn between her sense of duty and love produce profound artistry, and the dispute between Maggie and Stephen pulls us into each of their feelings. When Maggie says, 'I must not, cannot seek my own happiness by sacrificing others' (Book VI,

Chapter 11), it speaks volumes for the author's belief which had been fostered in her whole life. Similar remarks are repeated when Maggie and Stephen drift ashore on their way to elopement.

Although Maggie has been in a state of spiritual darkness for a long time, she has determined to say good-bye to him by this time. Her resolution still wavers under Stephen's endearing tones, but she says, 'I cannot marry you – I cannot take a good for myself that has been wrung out of their misery.' (Book VI, Chapter 14) These lines express her extreme moral pain and it is this morality that prevents the novel from becoming a cheap love story.

One of the notable characteristics of George Eliot's novels is that the fallible and more complex flesh-and-blood heroines are realistically and sympathetically described. She instigated a new movement in the history of English novels by presenting the psychological description of their inner life so analytically and realistically.

The author takes readers to the inner world of the heroines to empathise with them through their complicated situations.

After the author was acclaimed for *Adam Bede*, she became conscious of her influence and aware of her duty as a writer. She found her mission in elevating the human mind by expanding sympathies. On that account, her ultimate objective in describing the conflicts of Maggie and Stephen could be found in the wealth of spirituality and the triumph of humanity over animality.

The Mill on the Floss is a powerful and emotional story about the conflicts and the choice between duty and love. The individual and his or her environment interact dynamically as if they had a life and soul of their own. The vivid descriptions of the dense social structure support the story.

I have tried to cast a light on the various dilemmas of Maggie or Marian through this most autobiographical work and to read the author's message to the reader and the artistic effects in the novel, by linking Maggie's inner experience to the author's.

This story is very personal in a sense as it led the author to describe truthfully her own thoughts and emotions. The outcome is one of George Eliot's best-loved works.

About the Contributor

Mari Seaword is a UK based Japanese translator. Her translations include *The Ability to Write, the Ability to Think: Tsunesaburo Makiguchi's Composition Teaching Method* by Takao Ito, which is published in *Makiguchi Tsunesaburo in the Context of Language, Identity and Education* (Routledge, 2017) and a Japanese short story from 1917, *At Cape Kinosaki* by Naoya Shiga, for which she received a commendation from the John Dryden Translation Competition for 2010 - 2011.

She obtained her MA in English Literature from Soka University in Japan and gained her second MA in Translation from the University of Newcastle upon Tyne. She has a strong interest in literature, especially George Eliot and her contemporaries. Currently she is working as an in-house translator for a Japanese organisation in Scotland. She also voluntarily supports a UN non-governmental organisation who promotes peace, culture and education, based on the humanistic principles of Buddhism

Chapter 8

"Many Theresas" and "Angels":
Middlemarch and Mentoring Women

Angela Runciman

> "[Eliot's power] is at its highest in the mature
> *Middlemarch*, the magnificent book which
> with all its imperfections is one of the few
> English novels written for grown-up
> people."—
> from Virginia Woolf's essay, "George Eliot"[1]

It has been nearly 15 years since I first encountered
George Eliot's *Middlemarch*[2], and it seems in retrospect
that the intellectual struggles and desires of protagonist
Dorothea Brooke became clearer and more meaningful
as the years passed—as though I grew up alongside the
novel.

I still find Eliot intimidating, and larger than life. She
does not easily expose her vulnerabilities, though it is
so worth it when those pieces of her, and the deeply
beautiful complexities of human experience, emerge
briefly from the margins to reveal a profound human
truth. As I matured as a reader, thinker, and writer, I
began to detect how *Middlemarch* in particular asks for

---

[1] Virginia Woolf, "George Eliot," *Women and Writing*, edited by
Michéle Barrett, Harcourt, 1979.

[2] All references to Eliot's *Middlemarch* are from the Oxford edition
by David Carroll and Felicia Bonaparte, 1996.

a great deal of our close attention, as grains of much bigger ideas gradually appear for us, but only when we are ready to receive them.

In the course of writing this essay, I also realised how difficult it is to locate that personal connection to Eliot—she almost seems to resist the personal language I wanted to find to describe her significance in my life's work, since my relation to her has been primarily professional. My unavoidable turns to the academic seem reflective of the ways she represents that period in my life while I was still developing as a young scholar—and looking to those mentors and influences who would ultimately give my academic study its direction.

When I first read *Middlemarch* in Nancy Henry's Eliot seminar as a second-year master's student at Binghamton University, I was stopped in my tracks in a particular section which seemed to echo the German Romantic poet, Novalis, as well as the German literary-critic Walter Benjamin—both of whom I had studied with my dissertation director and dear friend, Gisela Brinker-Gabler. The initial flash of insight that I received from the novel led me to discover Eliot's immersion in German Romantic thought and her career as a critic and translator—followed by her career shift to fiction, which famously took place on her honeymoon and research tour in Germany with George Henry Lewes in 1854.

These ideas are the seeds which grew into my reading of Eliot as a European and Modern woman writer.

Looking back, this has revealed itself as a formative moment for my life's career direction, full of excitement and inspiration, in which the professional became deeply personal. Like the way in which St. Theresa lends mystical guidance to Dorothea in the novel, Eliot herself captured my attention in *Middlemarch*—and the rest gradually fell into place as my mentors guided me toward the philosophical connections with Benjamin that frame my doctoral work, and the lens through which I continue to view my research and reading of literature.

As I reached my dissertation conclusions about Eliot and the necessity of women's mentorship, it became apparent to me that my project became reflective of my own chosen network of women mentors who put me on my path as an academic.

Over the years, I have gained a great deal from the mentorship of women, whose guidance became more distinctly invaluable as I navigated the waters of academia as a first-generation college student. In a profession (like many others) where the pathways for women still sometimes seem uncharted, I have been very fortunate to know strong, pioneering women who pushed me and trusted my academic preparation more than I did myself.

The reward of engaging Eliot and Benjamin together, is to reveal the many ways in which their philosophically complex texts are alive, and call us to action. Sometimes it takes an emergent moment in one's own life to understand that kind of call, but they also show just how critically challenging that path to understanding can be without the right kind of guidance.

One of Benjamin's well-known writings is the "Angel of History,"[3] a powerless figure who despairingly looks on the "wreckage" of history as a "storm irresistibly

_____

[3] From Walter Benjamin's "Theses on the Philosophy of History," in *Illuminations*, edited by Hannah Arendt, and translated by Harry Zohn, Schocken Books, 1968, pp. 257-8.

propels him into the future." The Angel serves as an urgent reminder of the task of the historian to attend to hidden or marginalized stories—before the opportunity passes and they become impossible to recognize.

In the Prelude to *Middlemarch*, St. Theresa is introduced as a sort of guardian angel; her philosophical and feminist history hover over the text as the narrator celebrates, and at the same time, laments women's histories—in the hopes of rescuing Dorothea, a budding scholar, from her own tragic story:

> That Spanish woman who lived three hundred years ago, was certainly not the last of her kind. Many Theresas have been born who found for themselves no epic life wherein there was a constant unfolding of far-resonant action; perhaps only a life of mistakes, the offspring of a certain spiritual grandeur ill-matched with the meanness of opportunity; perhaps a tragic failure, which found no sacred poet and sank unwept into oblivion.... [T]o common eyes their struggles seemed mere inconsistency and formlessness; for these later-born Theresas were helped by no coherent social faith and order which could perform the function of knowledge for the ardently willing soul.
> (*Middlemarch* 3)

Both Eliot and Virginia Woolf evoke an especially urgent concern with the limitations of women's education and promote the notion of support between women in their essays and fiction. Most specifically, what shines through is the crucial necessity of mentorship of women by other women, in order to, as Eliot's narrator puts it, "perform the function of knowledge."

For Dorothea, "fed on meagre Protestant histories and on art chiefly of the handscreen sort," the unanswered questions of the past—the "gigantic broken revelations"—seem to beckon to her, but are too overwhelming and beyond her preparation (181).

Despite her strong desire to know, and St. Theresa's arguably strong desire to help her, Dorothea's lack of confidence about the "right" interpretations of art and history prevent her from realising her dreams of becoming a scholar in her own right—reflecting the catastrophic symptoms of nineteenth-century women's education which maintained patterns of control over women's lives and minds, and perpetuated expectations of servitude.

Through Dorothea's character, Eliot proposes that women really get to know themselves and learn how to help themselves—and each other—before taking on roles of service and care, including, and perhaps especially, marriage.

While St. Theresa's ecstasy was a mystical experience through which she received an all-encompassing love of God (which was criticized by the church establishment), St. Theresa's influence on Dorothea is more of a secret, spiritual partnership, as though St. Theresa is there right alongside her, lending a knowledge that is secular, intellectual, and sexual, all at once.

This profound flash of insight from St. Theresa, together with a recognition about her marriage, creates in Dorothea a "stupendous fragmentariness" which "[jars] her as with an electric shock" (180-1), ultimately giving her support to carry on and see value within herself as a knowing, intelligent individual, but not without continued frustration and difficulty working within the confines of conventional conduct.

Later in the novel, Dorothea's knowledge about marriage allows her to help Rosamond as she struggles through her own marriage crisis: the language signifying St. Theresa's ecstasy surrounds this private moment they share,[4] demonstrating the solidarity of Dorothea and Rosamond's commiseration, and, as Kathryn Bond Stockton argues, an erotic connection.[5]

This scene of women's mentorship—which Eliot somewhat "codes" into the narrative, as it challenges attitudes and standards of female behaviour—appears to shock both Dorothea and Rosamond, but also better prepares them for their lives and as women with a new found sense of themselves.

In both of these "outlined"[6] images of female mentorship, the frisson and feeling of longing which

---

[4] Rosamond's own "shock" is described as a "pang, as if a wound within her had been probed" (*Middlemarch* 747)—echoing St. Theresa's self-described ecstasy, translated: "It seemed to me this angel plunged the dart several times into my heart and that it reached deep within me. When he drew it out, I thought he was carrying off with him the deepest part of me; and he left me all on fire with great love of God" (as quoted in Carol Slade, *St. Teresa of Avila: Author of a Heroic Life*, U of California P, 1995, pp. 94-5)

[5] See Kathryn Bond Stockton, *God Between Their Lips: Desire Between Women in Irigaray, Brontë, and Eliot*, Stanford UP, 1994, pp. 242-3; Carol Slade also briefly discusses Teresa's significance in *Middlemarch* in her chapter 7 on psychoanalytic interpretations (144).

[6] In her book *Image in Outline: Reading Lou Andreas-Salomé*, Gisela Brinker-Gabler argues that the 19th-century writer and psychoanalyst Andreas-Salomé is concerned specifically with "'Woman's becoming,' which requires attention to women's life experiences and a remembering and rewriting of images" (14). Eliot's protagonists illustrate parallel concerns with "rewriting" the way we imagine women's lives, and their development as intellectual and sexual beings.

exudes from these encounters represents the urgency and necessity of support between women to help them realise the greatness they may have deep inside themselves—and to express the joys and sorrows that all human beings share, regardless of gender.

As Dorothea misses out on the kind of mentorship that may have more strongly helped her to realise her scholarly potential, I am reminded of the sacrifices of past generations of women—some of whom supported this first-generation college student to come this far—and I expect that feeling, along with the way I read Eliot and Dorothea, will keep evolving with age.

Despite the tragedy of her marriage choice to the old-fashioned scholar, Edward Casaubon, who declares himself to "live too much with the dead" and merely recycles old histories in his work (*Middlemarch* 16), Dorothea's endurance and reception of insight are Eliot's strongest messages that she embodied within herself the potential for a more remarkable, "epic life" (3).

As a realist and philosophical writer, I believe the limitations Eliot placed on her heroines are purposeful and depict the larger truths and losses that are part of women's history and experience—while also giving a sense of hope for the future. This message is just as relevant in 2019 as it was when Eliot began writing *Middlemarch* in 1869.

In the dark and disappointing days following the US election in 2016, I was filled with a profound sadness—but, thinking through Eliot and Dorothea, I also came around to a sense of hopefulness, that as we recover, these sacrifices more clearly begin to effect breaks in longstanding patterns to bring about change.

A few days following the election, Gisela and I changed our memory and the narrative of that week with celebrations of recent professional successes, including a "Career Champion" award for which I had nominated her—as well as her upcoming birthday.

I often think back on that week and remember those celebrations first, and how many more cracks Hillary Clinton smashed into that proverbial glass ceiling which I trust will ultimately give way. And then I think about Eliot, and my reading of Dorothea in *Middlemarch*, that amidst the limitations and ways in which things may fall short, the history of women springs eternal with hope for the future, and allows us to find solace to keep working, and hoping: "latent powers may find their long-waited opportunity; a past error may urge a grand retrieval" (*Middlemarch* 779).

About the Contributor

Angela E. Runciman is a faculty member in the Department of Comparative Literature at Binghamton University (SUNY, USA), where she is also completing her dissertation, "An (Un)historic Becoming: Reading George Eliot's *Middlemarch* with Walter Benjamin." Runciman teaches courses on topics such as Modern women writers, European Modernism, and a seminar on Eliot, Virginia Woolf, and Walter Benjamin.

She recently presented "Feeling (for) Knowledge: Conjuring the (Un)historic Constellations of St. Theresa and Dorothea in Eliot's *Middlemarch*" at the George Eliot Bicentenary Conference in Leicester in July 2019, for which she received a Humphreys Bursary Award; and "Undermining Nationalism and Recovering Marginalized Voices in Woolf's *Mrs Dalloway*" at the 29th annual International Conference on Virginia Woolf in June 2019, which is currently under review for publication. In 2014, Runciman chaired the organizing committee of the 22nd British Women Writers Conference held at Binghamton University. Memberships include the Council for European Studies at Columbia University, British Women Writers Association Executive Board, and International Virginia Woolf Society.

Part 3

Her Entirely Modern Views
New and Novel Takes on the Stories

Chapter 9

Intimations of Same-Sex Relationships in George Eliot's Fiction

Constance M. Fulmer

One of the many things about George Eliot's writing which intrigues me is the way she uses every character, every situation, and every artistic device to teach a moral lesson; an example of this is how she handles characters who are "different" or "other."

She frequently includes these characters and their interactions with those around them in order to teach timeless lessons about the need for love, acceptance, sympathy, and forgiveness. George Eliot creates characters whose nationalities and racial backgrounds are different from her own, characters with special needs, characters who have physical and mental disabilities, and characters who lean toward same-sex relationships.

By reading George Eliot's novels, we learn how to deal with our own "differences" and how to respond to the "differences" we see in others. She is amazing in her ability to create characters and situations which are totally relevant today and from which we can learn valuable lessons which are applicable in our own lives.

In recent years a number of critics have suggested that some of George Eliot's characters - both men and women - are sexually attracted to individuals of the same sex. The most intriguing thing about the idea to me is that the characters who are mentioned as having same-sex relationships are at the opposite ends of George Eliot's moral spectrum. On the good end of the spectrum are Daniel Deronda and Mordecai who are totally devoted to one another, and each of them is exemplary in being characterized by concern for others, empathy, and fellow-feeling. At the bad end of the spectrum are Tito Melema in *Romola* and Henleigh Grandcourt in *Daniel Deronda* - who are perhaps George Eliot's most morally depraved characters. Both Tito and Grandcourt are glaring examples of egotism, self-centeredness, and selfishness.

Tito is the most morally transgressive of all of George Eliot's characters. He betrays his father and Romola's father and has neither respect for the past nor a sense of responsibility to Romola, his illegitimate children, their mother, nor to any other person.

Tito obviously uses homosexual overtures to advance himself and has no conscience; he blatantly uses his good looks and sexual charm to win personal and political favour for himself. Even if George Eliot did not intend to portray Tito as sexually involved with Nello, Pucci, or Spini, there is an air of suspicion about his relationships with these men that implies same-sex attraction.

Nello is the barber who introduces Tito to Florence and whose barber shop provides a convenient meeting and gathering place for all of the men who are important in Tito's world. Nello plays with Tito's curls (130) and adores him; in one of the numerous scenes which involve flirtation and political intrigue, Nello refers to Tito as "the handsomest scholar in the world" (97).

Tito's effeminacy and egotism encourage Nello's voyeuristic fascination with Tito's person.

Giannozzo Pucci is a member of the Medicean party who woos Tito at dinner by "laying his hand on Tito's shoulder" and flattering him (346), and Tito is playing the lute for Pucci in a suggestive manner when Baldassarre, Tito's father, makes an unexpected appearance (348). Dolfo Spini is the leader of the opposition against Savonarola, and his attention to Tito -- such as his "affectionate pat on Tito's shoulder" (518) – certainly suggests more than the casual gesture of a comrade.

Henleigh Grandcourt in *Daniel Deronda* is also on this morally depraved end of George Eliot's spectrum of unwholesome behaviour. Grandcourt's questionable and suspicious loyalty to Lush, his right-hand man, raises suspicions of same-sex attraction.

When Grandcourt marries Gwendolen Harleth, he promises her that he will let Lush go if his presence is not pleasing to her (182); however, Lush's reappearance is a telling indication of the crushing dominance that Grandcourt has over Gwendolen, and it is clear that Grandcourt is totally dependent on him (305).

And Lush says of Grandcourt, "I'm attached to him, of course, I've given up everything else for the sake of keeping by him, and it has lasted a good fifteen years now" (280).

The relationship between Grandcourt and Lush is similar to the one between Harold Transome and his man Dominic in *Felix Holt*. Harold says that Dominic is "cook, valet, major domo, and secretary all in one, and what's more he's an affectionate fellow – I can trust to his attachment" (37).

The negative aura of shared secrets as well as a questionable past characterises both of these relationships.

On the good end of George Eliot's moral spectrum, Daniel Deronda is the epitome of what George Eliot considered to be an ideal example of moral behaviour.

Even though Daniel is self-effacing and insecure about his own identity, he reaches out unselfishly with a sincere desire to help the two males who are hinted to be of sexual interest to him – Hans Myrick and Mordecai. In the same generous way he reaches out to Mirah Lapidoth, who becomes his wife, and to Gwendolyn Harleth and to everyone whose life touches his.

George Eliot says that between Deronda and Mordecai there was "so intense a consciousness as if they had been declared lovers" (495).

We cannot deny that in creating Daniel Deronda George Eliot is aware of gender roles and that she gives him both feminine and masculine characteristics. George Eliot's narrator says that "Deronda was moved by an affectionateness such as we are apt to call feminine, disposing him to yield in ordinary details, while he had a certain inflexibility of judgment, and independence of opinion, held to be rightfully masculine" (322).

In *Daniel Deronda* Daniel is not only emotionally dependent on Mordecai, he is very devoted to his dear friend Hans Myrick and is so anxious to help Hans pass his examinations at Cambridge that in doing so he fails his own exams (462). Hans confides in Daniel his fascination with and attraction to Mirah Lapidoth, and it is only after Daniel realizes that Hans is interested in

Mirah that Daniel admits the depth and extent of his own feelings toward Mirah (462-63).

So in having both her best characters and her worst characters exemplify tendencies which are stereotypically associated with homosexuality, George Eliot is not necessarily advocating same-sex relationships but is illustrating the extremes of attitude and behaviour which define her moral message. She understands that she can most effectively show the difference between extreme selfishness and utter unselfishness by using the ways human beings respond and reach out to one another in behaviour which is generally associated with sexual attraction.

Throughout George Eliot's writings, there are also other pairs of characters whose relationships are coloured and enhanced by the aura of same-sex attraction.

Bartle Massey mentors Adam Bede in ways similar to but much less extreme than the way Mordecai mentors Daniel. Bartle Massey serves as Adam's teacher and spiritual guide. He conducts a night school for Adam Bede, the carpenter, and other working men. He is very dismissive of women and the need for them and says that he will never be fool enough to let any woman into his home except his dog Vixen (238). And Bartle lovingly watches with Adam during Hetty's trial (422) and expresses his concern and desire to commune with Adam in every phase of his suffering (428).

While Bartle Massey has a positive impact on Adam Bede's life, Silas Marner's friend William Dane plays a very negative part in his story.

Before Silas Marner comes to Raveloe, his very close friend ruins Silas's reputation and takes the young woman to whom Silas is betrothed to be his own wife.

The narrator remarks: "among the members of his church there was one young man, a little older than himself, with whom he had long lived in such close friendship that it was the custom of their Lantern Yard brethren to call them David and Jonathan" (10).

This dear friend, William Dane, steals the church money and sets up the circumstances so that Silas Marner is charged with the crime. The betrayal by his cherished friend causes Silas to leave the church, move to far away Raveloe, and to cut himself off from society.

In George Eliot's short story "The Lifted Veil," two very close same-sex relationships contribute to the sinister atmosphere and strange circumstances. The main character Latimer is an odd and very sensitive child (5) who in his youth has one intimate friendship with a young man named Charles Meunier (8). When Latimer learns that Meunier is coming for a visit, he feels that his presence will be "like a transient resurrection into a happier pre-existence" (37).

This friend appears in time to bring about the "scientific" experiment in which Meunier reanimates the corpse of Mrs. Archer. Her revival gives her the opportunity to share the secret that Latimer's wife Bertha plans to kill him (42).

Significantly after Mrs. Archer was hired as a maid to Bertha, the two become suspiciously close; Mrs. Archer "rapidly became a favourite with her mistress" (35), and the women shared many confidences.

On the good end of the moral spectrum, in "Janet's Repentance" one of the *Scenes of Clerical Life*, George Eliot refers to the kisses between Janet and Mrs. Pettifer as "such kisses as seal a new and closer bond between the helper and the helped" (78).

And one sexually charged scene between Rosamond and Dorothea in *Middlemarch* is full of significant looks, hand pressing, and physical proximity. This scene is important to the moral growth of both Rosamond and Dorothea; ironically their encounter leads Dorothea to become more aware of her love for and commitment to Will Ladislaw whom she marries.

George Eliot provides several hints that Will Ladislaw himself has transgendered attributes; for example, he is described as a slim young fellow with his girl's complexion (610); and when Bulstrode's secrets are found out, Ladislaw "wept like a woman" (624).

The degree to which George Eliot understood every aspect of human nature – including same-sex relationships – is truly amazing. She clearly realized that reaching out to another person in a meaningful way – whether for selfish or unselfish reasons – involved gestures and sharing which had sexual overtones.

In many ways, George Eliot's depictions of same-sex relationships are integral aspects of her moral message which will stand the test of time. Perhaps on the occasion of George Eliot's two-hundredth birthday, we can say of her what Ben Jonson said of Shakespeare that she is not for an age but for all time.

References

Eliot, George. *Daniel Deronda*, edited by Terence Cave. Penguin Books, 1995.

Felix Holt, edited by Lynda Mugglestone. Penguin Books, 1995.

The Lifted Veil and Brother Jacob. Oxford World's Classics, edited by Helen Small. Oxford University Press, 1999.

Middlemarch, edited by Rosemary Ashton. Penguin Books, 1994.

Romola, edited by Dorothea Barrett. Penguin Books, 1996.

Scenes of Clerical Life, edited by Graham Handley. J. M. Dent, 1994.

Silas Marner, edited by David Carroll. Penguin Books, 1996.

Fulmer, Constance M. *George Eliot's Moral Aesthetic*. Routledge, 2019.

"Hints of Same-Sex Attraction and Transgender Traits in George Eliot's Characters." *George Eliot: Interdisciplinary Essays*, edited by Jean Arnold and Lila Marz Harper. Palgrave, 2019, 247-65.

About the Contributor

Constance M. Fulmer is Professor of Victorian Literature and holds the Blanche E. Seaver Chair in English Literature at Seaver College, Pepperdine University in Malibu, California. Routledge has recently published her *George Eliot's Moral Aesthetic: Compelling Contradictions*, 2019.

She is working on an edition of primary sources related to Edith J. Simcox with Margaret E. Barfield. She and Margaret Barfield edited *A Monument to the Memory of George Eliot: Edith J. Simcox's Autobiography of a Shirtmaker* (Garland, 1998).

She has published several articles on George Eliot and on Edith Simcox and an annotated bibliography of George Eliot criticism (G.K. Hall). She serves on the board of the Victorian Interdisciplinary Studies Association of the Western United States and is active in the British Women Writers Association.

Her Ph.D. is from Vanderbilt University in Nashville, Tennessee. She has been at Pepperdine since 1990 and served as Associate Dean of Seaver College from 2007 to 2016 and for eight years as Divisional Dean.

Her article "Hints of Same-Sex Attraction and Transgender Traits in George Eliot's Characters" in *George Eliot: Interdisciplinary Essays*, edited by Jean

Arnold and Lila Marz Harper, Palgrave, 2019, provides a more extensive treatment of the ideas she discusses here.

Chapter 10

George Eliot at Home

Dr Ailsa Boyd

There are many homes in the novels of George Eliot, from clergymen's ugly lodgings in the Midlands countryside, poor weavers' cottages with bags of gold hidden beneath the bricks, to the grand Gothick buildings of the landowners with plasterwork like 'petrified lace', and Palladian mansions with glittering, mirrored boudoirs. To the Victorian reader, the furniture and decoration of these rooms provided an extra layer of characterisation, which we can access with some knowledge of interior decoration.

Eliot's themes of morality, character and history interlock with many issues raised by the design reformers of the 1850s, whose ideas led to the Arts and Crafts movement of the 1880s. This widespread cultural debate began with concern over rapid industrialisation and the production of mass-market goods, and involved issues of style, morality and truth.

In simple terms, the Victorians could look at how you decorated your home and work out what sort of person you were.

The domestic interior was also widely understood to be a woman's natural sphere, so how women acted in the home was also up for scrutiny. This cultural background provides a key to enable us to 'read' the interiors of Eliot's novels as aspects of character. Her own home was designed by Owen Jones, a leading design reformer, who was the superintendent of works for the Great Exhibition in 1851, and she shared his theories on the importance of good design for a happy life.

Although Eliot does not furnish the homes in her novels in great detail, with just a few words she creates memorable scenes that firmly locate the characters. The eponymous Dorlcote Mill on the river Floss has a worm-eaten, cobwebby attic where young Maggie retreats from the 'bitter sorrows of childhood' to hit her Fetish. But the family home takes on a 'new strange bareness' after the bankruptcy sale when Mrs Tulliver's 'chany' and cloths that she spun herself are all sold.

This relationship of money to how houses are furnished runs throughout Eliot's novels, providing a commentary on the morality of those who save, borrow, inherit, or sometimes steal. The poorest buildings can be homes in ways a mansion cannot, if they are filled with loving family, or as Mr Glegg notices, 'We get a deal o' useless things about us, only because we've got the money to spend'.

In *Adam Bede*, the evening scenes in the adjoining 'meagrely furnished rooms' of Hetty and Dinah demonstrate their different natures – Hetty admiring her beautiful hair and eyelashes in the tarnished mirror, Dinah looking out of her window, over the fields, thinking about the problems of others. In *Middlemarch* Rosamond's dreams of marriage are mainly taken up with imagining her future drawing room in various styles of furniture, and we can foresee the disaster of her marriage to Lydgate in their shared feeling that 'good housekeeping consisted simply in ordering the best of everything'. The epitome of this conspicuous consumption in *Daniel Deronda* is Quetcham Hall, the home of the *nouveau riches* Arrowpoints, 'That magnificent mansion, fitted with regard to the greatest expense . . .'

The famous pier-glass metaphor in *Middlemarch* has a domestic origin, inspired by Eliot looking at 'your ugly furniture'. By the 1860s large mirrors with gilt rococo frames hung on the wall piers between windows were out of fashion for their style and flashiness. But most impressively, Eliot explains the narrative method of the novel and her doctrine of sympathy by using only a cloth, candle and piece of glass. She describes how the pier-glass rubbed by a housemaid 'will be minutely and multitudinously scratched in all directions; but place now against it a lighted candle as a centre of illumination, and lo! the scratches will seem to arrange themselves in a fine series of concentric circles'.

Focusing on one character can give a false sense of perspective, so the novel gives us many different viewpoints. But this also highlights the delusion of the self-centred person, for 'these things are a parable. The scratches are events, and the candle is the egoism of any person'. Dorothea will struggle out of this self-centred existence, to understand, through sympathy, the other characters in the novel, act in their interests and attain happiness for herself.

When she moved to London in 1850, Eliot lived in rented rooms, and did so even after she and Lewes 'eloped'. It was only in 1863, after the publication of *Romola*, that Eliot was wealthy enough to buy a white villa with a large garden in St John's Wood, called The Priory. This would be the venue for the famous Sunday afternoon salons, where Eliot and Lewes entertained the literary, scientific, musical and intellectual society of the day, on their own terms. The double drawing room was decorated to the height of reformed fashion by Owen Jones. Eliot's partnership with Lewes was famously unconventional by contemporary standards, but as perhaps the richest novelist of the time, she was able to reverse the gender roles by being the one who paid for the expensive decoration. It was quite an undertaking, and we know that wallpaper was specially made, and the scaffolding and paint forced them to remove to lodgings for some weeks.

Jones had published *The Grammar of Ornament* in 1856, which became an essential design textbook for the new schools of art and design throughout Britain. He identified the essential elements for good design: 'fitness, proportion, harmony', which were watchwords of the design reform movement, who wanted to banish the floral carpets, overstuffed sofas and mahogany curlicues of the typical Victorian middle-class home.

His wallpaper was characterised by geometric patterns, sometimes derived from Eastern designs, with dark and light colours arranged in carefully considered harmonies. Jones believed that good, honest and beautiful design was essential for a healthy society.

Eliot agreed with this in her review of *The Grammar*: 'the subtle relation between all kinds of truth and fitness in our life forbids that bad taste should ever be harmless'. Throughout her novels she demonstrates the relationship between well-being and surroundings, as part of her doctrine of sympathy.

In accordance with the most fashionable taste, Eliot's own drawing room had curtains on simple rails without pelmets, furniture that was not overstuffed, an old-fashioned basket grate, and wallpaper with a flat pattern of foliage, giving visitors an overall impression of modest harmony and taste.

Dorothea in *Middlemarch* believes that 'life in cottages might be happier than ours, if they were real houses fit for human beings from whom we expect duties and affections'. She decides to build homes for the workers on her estate, but what the other characters think is a 'fad', is part of her search for a purpose, in a society where women were only meant to be wives and mothers.

The importance of the project was evident to Eliot, the estate manager's daughter, who was also friends with the philanthropist Octavia Hill, who turned building cottages for the poor into a profession in the 1860s.

But Dorothea's motivations also anticipate the design reform movement, with her plans to modify 'men's moods and habits' and improve the lives of the poor through beautiful if simple, and practical surroundings. Her designs come from J.C. Loudon's *A Manual of Cottage Gardening, Husbandry, and Architecture* of 1830, which contains detailed plans for practical and modern cottages with a washhouse, cesspool, oven and flue, even a beehouse and pigeon place.

Dorothea's own room is the setting for an emotional turning point in the novel. On her marriage to the much older Casaubon, she chose his mother's boudoir in Lowick Manor for her own space. It is decorated with old-fashioned blue furniture which is 'thin-legged and easy to upset' and an evocative tapestry on the wall of 'a blue-green world with a pale stag in it'.

The pale, faded room is highly romantic, nostalgic and feminine, but the female ancestors with their powdered hair in the portrait miniatures prove supportive during Dorothea's despair at being 'shut up in that stone prison at Lowick'.

After Ladislaw's apparent rejection of her love, she spends a long night in this room in sorrowful meditation, but in the morning she is able to look out the window and see a family walking across the fields, and 'she felt the largeness of the world'.

This is sympathy in action, nurtured by her surroundings, enabling her to see beyond herself to the struggles of the world and realise her place within it.

The homes of morally admirable characters in Eliot often embody the values of honesty and generosity.

Bob Jakin generously gives Tom Tulliver lodgings in his 'queer old house pierced with surprising passages', which is scrupulously clean and a tiny home for his growing family. Shabby, unostentatious furnishings demonstrate the importance of family history and a sense of rootedness.

In *Middlemarch*, Farebrother's 'old-fashioned parlour' is filled with furniture and pictures 'with another grade of age' layered upon them, like the old chairs with 'some lingering red silk damask with slits in it'.

Perhaps this is the best home in the novel, matriarchal, simple and sustaining, for Farebrother embodies emotional far-sightedness and generosity, gives good advice to all, and with his sister, propels the love plot towards resolution.

When Gwendolen's bankrupt family move into Offendene in *Daniel Deronda*, with its worn red satin chairs, 'venerable knick-knacks', and all the fires lit to welcome them, it seems like a refuge. However, in a turn worthy of a ghost story, the walls of the house warn the 'spoiled child' Gwendolen of her future troubles, with a mysterious hinged panel opening to reveal a dead face and a fleeing figure. This again springs open when she is performing a *tableau vivant*, terrifying her into a piercing cry and collapse in front of her audience.

Gwendolen is just one of several characters in the novel searching for a home, which she realises is not a mansion filled with paintings and diamonds, but a refuge built from love and family.

Whether by choice or design, Mirah, Mordecai and the mesmerising Alcharisi travel around, rootless, living in hotels and lodgings. Their stories all intersect around Deronda, who will throw off the curse of the Wandering Jew, with his quest for a Jewish homeland.

The many richly decorated mansions in the novel are merely backgrounds, and it is the smaller family homes like the Meyricks' in Chelsea, where the cheap engravings on the wall and shabby furniture are worth nothing to anyone else who doesn't know the family associations.

In Eliot's last novel, domesticity has become a metaphor for something larger, and in this narrow home 'there was space and apparatus for a wide-glancing, nicely-select life, open to the highest things'.

With music, poetry and beauty, the love and respect of family life can make a collection of furniture in rooms into a home that will nurture its inhabitants to see beyond themselves.

Only then can we conquer the trials that life inevitably throws at us and move beyond grief and pain, as Gwendolen assures her mother, 'Don't be afraid. I shall live. I mean to live'.

About the contributor

Dr Ailsa Boyd is an independent writer, lecturer and curator, based in Glasgow, researching 19th century art, design and literature. She has published on manuals of household taste, Beatrix Whistler as a paradigmatic woman artist, Edith Wharton's interior design, and the literary afterlives of Henry James's Lamb House.

https://ailsaboyd.wordpress.com

Chapter 11

George Eliot's Earliest Story:
Edward Neville and Its Source Book

Akiko Higuchi

At the age of 14, Mary Ann Evans, who was to become George Eliot, wrote her first known fiction and to aficionados of her writing it is very interesting and quite intriguing. It also revealed how even in her early life she was a painstaking researcher.

She also signed it Marianne Evans which is our first known record of her using that as her name.

The piece *Edward Neville*, is just a few pages of her notebook which was discovered by chance.

My purpose is to illustrate with examples how Marianne Evans was inspired by and depended on William Coxe, *An Historical Tour in Monmouthshire*[1] as her principal source[2], when she wrote *Edward Neville*. You can see the full text in Haight's biography, starting at page 552. My main text here, is Juliet

---

1. William Coxe. *An Historical Tour in Monmouthshire.* Illustrated with Views by Sir R. C. Hoare, Bart. A New Map of the County and Other Engravings. 2 vols. London: T. Cadell, Jun. and W. Davies, in the Strand, 1801. Print.
2. Marianne Evans. "Edward Neville". Appendix I: George Eliot's School Notebook. Gordon S. Haight. *George Eliot: A Biography.* Oxford UP, 1968. Print, p. 17.

McMaster's *Edward Neville*[3] though, I do refer to Coxe's travel book, I may refer to Haight's biography.

Using the descriptions and the engraved pictures in Coxe's book, she could create the figures of the main characters such as Edward Neville, Henry Marten, Sir Verner Mordaunt, and Miss Mary Mordaunt, as well as the places, including Chepstow Castle and Piercefield House.

Overview of *Edward Neville*

At the age of 14, Evans had started to write a historical romance between Edward and Mary. It has some hints of the possibility of it developing into a romance where Edward and Mary may marry and live happily forever, like a fairy tale.

For this to happen, however, Edward must have to turn into a Royalist or Mary had to become a republican. Yet, Edward had been educated thoroughly by his anti-Royalist uncle for more than 10 years, and Mary had a firm Royalist father.

While writing, Evans will have been aware that the political principles of Edward and Mary would never coincide.

Besides, Mary stays silent till the end of the story, and her feelings towards Edward have not been expressed by word at all. We only know that she accepted small gifts from Edward until she was fifteen and he was eighteen. The reader cannot surmise what feelings she had continued to have entertained towards him for these eight years. Besides, who can tell whether Mary,

---

3. *Edward Neville*. Ed. Juliet McMaster and others. Illustrated by Juliet McMaster. Sydney: Juvenilia Press, 2009. Print.

now twenty-three years old, has been married or had died?

Edward must have recognized that he and Mary could never be able to even see each other. This may be why "a tear started to his eye, ... and a deep sigh burst from his heart" (Evans, p. 3). The reader knows the fact that he and his uncle had been forbidden by Sir Verner to visit Mary any more. That is to say, he cannot visit Piercefield House not only at this time, but also in the future. Therefore there will be no possibility of their meeting, and certainly not marrying.

The last question that Evans left us is why she stopped the story unfinished at this point even without a full stop. Since theoretically there would be no possibility of continuing the love story, she must have been obliged to give up writing, or she simply lost interest, although McMaster suggests us that it was Evans's "conscientious qualm" (p. xx) that forced her to stop writing.

Marianne Evans' Research

Even at age 14, Evans was meticulous about creating depth in her characters and placing them exactly. In the rest of this article I illustrate this and show the care that she took.

Why did Evans call the hero "Edward Neville"?

Because there were several Edward Nevills (without a final e) in the pedigree of a Welsh family that Coxe had associated with the lords of Abergavenny (pp. 180+ and 180++), and Evans clearly wanted to connect her fictional young hero with the noble family.

Who was Henry Marten (1602-80)[4]?

In her story, Marten is Edward's uncle, aged about 70. Actually, however, he was 48 years old in 1650 when Evans's story took place. He was a real, republican MP, whose character and behaviour are described in detail by Coxe (pp. 378-391).

In 1649, he, along with Oliver Cromwell and 57 other people, signed the warrant for the execution of King Charles I. According to Evans, this was why he was confined in Chepstow Castle. However, she was not correct in her historical understanding, because in 1650, just after the execution of Charles I in 1649, the republicans occupied the Castle during the Puritan Revolution. Historically, it was impossible that Marten could be confined in the Castle as a prisoner, in the Marten's Tower, which has been so called.

Evans must have read Coxe's descriptions on Marten, but as a juvenile authoress, she will have contrived her own story between Edward and his uncle. In her story, Edward needed to find a refuge in his uncle's prison.

Who is Sir Verner Mordaunt in her fiction?

Fictional Sir Verner Mordaunt in the story was created from two sources that Coxe wrote about.

One was the anecdote about Mr. Thomas Lewis, a royalist in the 17th century, who actually lived at St. Pierre near the Castle. He was a warm-hearted man, often inviting Henry Marten to his table (Coxe, p. 389) to console him and hoping to change him into a royalist.

---

4. Sarah Barber. *A Revolutionary Rogue: Henry Marten and the English Republic.* Thrupp · Stroud · Gloucestershire: Sutton Publishing Limited, 2000. Print.

The other source was Valentine Morris in the gorgeous Piercefield House in Chepstow who later went downhill miserably (Coxe, p. 392).

Evans combined these two figures into Sir Verner Mordaunt at Piercefield House.

Sr Walter Scott was one of Evans's favourite novelists and she had known *The Pirate*[5] since her childhood. This could have been another reason why Evans named her main fictional family "Mordaunt."

Who is Mary Mordaunt?

The heroine of *Edward Neville* came from two sources in Coxe's book.

Evans describes "Mary Mordaunt" as a fictional girl in the 17th century: "She [Mary Mordaunt] was the daughter [of] Sir Verner Mordaunt who had for many years resided in the beautiful mansion of Piercefield" (*Edward Neville*, p. 14).

The other source is Miss Mary Mordaunt, a historical lady in the 18th century, one century later, whom Evans read about in Coxe's book (p. 392). "About 1752, he [Valentine Morris (1727 –89)] espoused Miss Mary Mordaunt, and fixed his residence at Piercefield" (p. 392). It is a pity that her later life was a very miserable one.[6]

Therefore, it was Evans's imagination that combined the fictional Mary Mordaunt, the invented daughter of Sir Verner Mordaunt, whose model was Mr. Thomas Lewes at St. Pierre in the 17th century, with a real lady,

---

[5] Walter Scott, The Pirate. London: Blackwood, Scott & Company, n. d. Print.
[6] Haight p. 562

Miss Mary Mordaunt, later Mrs. Mary Morris, the wife of Valentine Morris, in the 18th century.

Evans clearly read these two anecdotes in Coxe's book as her sources for Miss Mary Mordaunt in *Edward Neville*.

Are there any typical similarities between Coxe's and Evans's descriptions?

There are many similar phrases and sentences. Here are some of them:

> Coxe: He [Henry Marten] possessed good talents (p. 379).
> Evans: Henry Marten ... possessed great talent (p. 4),

> Coxe: ... by espousing a rich widow (p. 379),
> Evans: ... he early in life married a rich widow (p. 4),

> Coxe: Hence he united with Harrington, Sydney, Wildman, Nevill and others, who denied the truth of revelation (p. 379).
> Evans: ... joined with several public characters of the time in openly denying the truths of revelation (p. 4).

> Coxe: When the temper of the times enabled him to disclose his sentiments with less restraint, Marten added disdain and insult to hatred of royalty (p. 380).
> Evans: When the temper of the times enabled him to disclose his sentiments without restraint, he added disdain and insult to dislike of the King (p. 4).

Coxe: Marten ... was present when the sentence was pronounced, and signed the warrant of death (p. 384).

Evans: ... and eventually with his own hand signed the warrant for that unhappy monarch's execution (p. 4):

Here are their sentences describing how Marten had a narrow escape from the death penalty at the Restoration in 1660:

Coxe: "At the restoration ... After pleading a misnomer✻, (p. 387) ... he obtained on condition of perpetual imprisonment. He was first confined in the tower, but soon removed to the castle of Chepstow" (p. 389):
✻Being excepted and indicted as Henry Marten, he urged that his name was Harry Marten; his signature on the king's warrant is Hen. Marten.

Evans: "He however escaped the just punishment of his crime by pleading a misnomer, he having been called in the Indictment "Henry Marten", whereas his real name was Harry. He was, however, found guilty, and confined for life in the Castle of Chepstow" (p. 4).

How did Evans know the geographical detail of the places, including Chepstow Castle?

Coxe's book includes many engravings of Chepstow Castle, such as pp. 365+, 366+, 370+, 372+, and 378+ (The Tower). These images must have stirred up her imagination to actualize the scenes in her story.

Did Evans also find engravings of Piercefield House?

She will have found one on p. 396+ (a far view) and another on p. 398+ (a map). They must have stimulated her imagination with Coxe's verbal descriptions of how gorgeous the mansion was.

Books

Akiko Higuchi. *The Brontës and Music*, 2 vols. Tokyo: Yushodo Press, 2008. (With a CD of *Anne Brontë's Song Book* and *Branwell Brontë's Flute Book*)

Text by David Ross; Illustrated by Virginia Gray. *Greyfriars Bobby*. Trans. Akiko Higuchi. Chiba: Alba-shobo, 2011. Print.

Marianne Evans, *Edward Neville*. Part I: Trans. Tsuneharu Higuchi and Akiko Higuchi; Part II: written by Akiko Higuchi by her on-the-spot survey. Tokyo: Sairyu-sha, 2011.

This book was chosen as "one of the Selected Books by the Library Society of Japan".

Alan H. Adamson, *Mr Charlotte Brontë*. Trans, Akiko Higuchi, Tokyo: Sairyu-sha, 2015.

This book was chosen as "one of the Selected Books by the Library Society of Japan".

Jolien Janzing, *De Meester*. Trans. Paul Vincent into English from Dutch. *Charlotte Brontë's Secret Love*. Trans. Akiko Higuchi into Japanese, e-book, 2017.

About the Contributor

Akiko Higuchi graduated from Tsuda College, 1958 and was awarded the Sarah de Ford Prize. She gained her MA in 1960 when she graduated from Gakushuin University. In 1973-75 she became a part-time teacher at Gakushuin Girls' Junior and Senior High School and became a full time teacher there between 1975-2000. She was also a part-time lecturer at Gakushuin

University between 1978 and 2000, as well as a part-time lecturer at Keio University between 1973-2000.

She was a visiting scholar at Cambridge University between 1988-89. From 2000, she was appointed a professor at The International University of Kagoshima, and then became a professor at the Graduate School of the International University of Kagoshima. In 2006 she was awarded a Litt. D from Gakushuin University.

Chapter 12

Opium and Addiction in *Silas Marner*

Kathleen McCormack

In 1994, American comedian, author, and filmmaker Steve Martin wrote and starred in a movie update of George Eliot's 1863 novel *Silas Marner* that he called *A Simple Twist of Fate*. Like Eliot's Silas, Martin's reclusive protagonist Michael McCann enjoys hoarding coins, in his case Franklin Mint-type collectibles. But Martin also updates Eliot's Silas by adding alcohol to his character's evening ritual of fondling his coins. Although Silas finds drugless satisfaction in his golden guineas, McCann enjoys his coins while downing shots of brown liquor one by one.

In *Silas Marner* George Eliot creates her most hopelessly addicted character in Molly Farren Cass: the ex-barmaid "enslaved" (NY: Penguin 1968, 112) by opium, whom the village squire's son Godfrey has secretly married during a binge engineered by his younger brother Dunsey. But Eliot moves beyond this obviously addicted character to add a village-full of daily drinkers at every level of the local hierarchy: from Jem Rodney the poacher, to Ben Winthrop the wheelwright and Dr. Kimble the apothecary, to Squire Cass himself.

Indeed Eliot's narratives generally reveal a grasp of addictive behaviour unusual during her period but entirely familiar to ours. In *Silas Marner*, she expands her range of addictions beyond alcohol and opium, the main drugs of her day, to include additional and most often drugless activities. Silas's hoarding, his weaving, Dunsey Cass's gambling, and even the conversation both at the Rainbow public house and at the village Squire's Open Houses all depend on the habitual repetition of some small-scale act or anecdote.

Hence the narrator proposes that many small repeated actions, endlessly pursued, carry the potential for addiction, observing of Silas's solitary pleasures: "Do we not while away moments of inanity or fatigued waiting by repeating some trivial movement or sound, until the repetition has bred a want, which is incipient habit?" (67) This want-turned-habit exemplifies Eliot's advanced awareness of dependencies on drugless as well as intoxicating substances or activities.

Eliot also enlarges her stock of intoxicants through metaphors she applies to a variety of behaviours. She brings Silas's hoarding into the realm of more usual addictions through the metaphor applied to his counting, calling his habit "golden wine" (72) for which he "thirsts." Described throughout the novel as "tankards" (73, 121, 211), the three men in the Cass family begin drinking first thing in the morning. The Raveloe villagers believe Dunsey's selfishness makes him likely to "enjoy his drink the more when other people went dry" (73), but that Godfrey has the merits of "a pot o' good ale" (160). Metaphors of intoxicants represent both faults and virtues (but mostly faults) in the characters in *Silas Marner*.

One of the many less obvious but, I think, therefore more interesting metaphors related to addiction concerns the name of the young Squire Cass. In 19th-Century Britain, shops sold opium legally over the counter and, together with alcohol, it made up 97% of the popular tonics, many of them marketed primarily to women and for children. According to Terry Parssinen, estimates of the ingestion of sweetened tincture of opium ran as high as 12,000 doses consumed by the children in Coventry in 1862 (*Secret Passions, Secret Remedies: Narcotic Drugs in British Society 1820-1930* Philadelphia: Institute for the Study of Human Issues, Inc., 1983).

By mid-century the most popular brand, Godfrey's Cordial, had become generic for children's opium. While his secret wife depends on daily opium doses at plot level, Godfrey Cass goes by a name known throughout Britain as an opium-based tonic for children.

Of all George Eliot's novels, *Silas Marner* has probably gathered the largest number of post-Victorian readers because of its frequent appearance on secondary school English Lit syllabi. But veterans of such reading lists, possibly bored to death by the hermit/miser during their teenage years, can anticipate the pleasures of re-reading Eliot's novels from an adult perspective: discovering the joke missed the first time around, recognizing the irony of a previously puzzling statement, and or possessing the patience to carry on through some of the narrator's subtle, complex, and sometimes very long sentences.

Along with these interpretive benefits for grownups, whether first timers or re-readers, only the luckiest of our contemporaries have led lives innocent of complications generated by someone's addiction. For this majority, Eliot provides her addicted characters a theory of recovery, again with some current familiarity.

Everywhere in her fiction Eliot creates addicted characters, her early story "Janet's Repentance" narrates Janet's recovery from alcoholism in patterns most recognizable today. Janet depends on absolute abstinence, a responsible sponsor in the clergyman Mr. Tryan, and reliance on a power higher than herself in Mr. Tryan's Evangelicalism.

Unlike Janet, when Silas loses all his coins to theft, he must go cold turkey from his addictive hoarding. Meanwhile, however, the sympathetic responses of his neighbours begin his integration within the community whose members, however flawed themselves, help curtail the isolation which has nourished his addiction.

His recovery takes a giant step when the child of Molly and the young Squire Cass wanders away from her drugged mother, who is dying in the snow, and into Silas's cottage where her golden curls first strike him as a return of his stolen gold. But Eppie's arrival does more for him. It replaces the repetitious habits of addiction with the adaptations he must contrive in order to deal with the needs of Eppie's ever-changing little life.

As Eppie grows, each day brings Silas a new challenge of parenthood that differs from its predecessors. His consultations with maternal neighbour Dolly Winthrop not only help him develop new strategies for dealing with Eppie's capers, but help revive Silas's lost spirituality. She encourages his becoming part of the village congregation thus reintroducing him to faith in a supreme being at the same time he is joining his neighbours in community.

Philosophers from Plato to Derrida have proposed the potential addictiveness of reading and writing themselves, sometimes presenting ink as an intoxicating substance. In *Silas Marner*, on the other hand, the spoken rather than the written word carries the addictive potential.

The conversations among the villagers, depending on social class, take place at either of two locations: the gentry meet and eat and talk at Squire Cass's New Year's Party while the humbler Ravelovians drink and talk at the village pub, the Rainbow.

The talk in both these locations depends on the repetition necessary to the transmission of oral tradition. At the holiday party at the Red House (with its pub-like name) the guests spend their time "paying each other old-established compliments in sound traditional phrases, passing well-tried personal jokes" (158) and engaging in "the annual Christmas talk" (141). In Raveloe's proto-literate culture, even the socially elevated characters have not abandoned repetitive oral tradition.

Eliot devotes two full chapters to the chat at the Rainbow, very little of it new to the company. Instead, the villagers repeat the story of the Lammeters' flawed wedding ritual, narrating an event from a generation ago. They also savour the familiar narrative they call "Cliff's Holiday," a ghost story that accounts for the availability of the country house the Lammeters come to occupy.

Dunsey Cass finds his motivation for seeking money in Silas's cottage in anticipation of telling his story to "a select circle at the Rainbow" (86) . The narrative potential at the public house offers an important supplement to the lure of the contents of the quart pots.

Nineteenth-Century temperance movements often blamed publicans for widespread drunkenness. Not only did they sell the alcohol, they drank along with their customers and participated in the talk. Mr. Snell at the Rainbow presides over his pub when, drawing on his authority as landlord, he cuts short any conversational conflicts with his declaration that the "Rainbow's the Rainbow" (97), articulating a sentence almost meaningless because of the tautology of repetition.

In proto-literate cultures, such as that of Raveloe, repetition allows the passing on of narrative through oral tradition alongside the budding literacy of the period, much of it confined to Sabbatarian Bible reading. At the Rainbow, intemperance results from repetition (repeated elbow bending) but it also causes the kind of ceaseless repetitions that try the patience of the non-drinker. Repetition is both cause and effect of intoxication.

Talking, hoarding, weaving, gambling, and alcohol thus extend Raveloe addictions far beyond the opium that destroys Molly. Steve Martin's revival of abstemious Silas in the drinker Michael McCann recognizes Eliot's inclusions of a variety of repetitious activities as addictions.

Meanwhile *Silas Marner* itself does not encourage addictive reading. Whereas Eliot published most of her other (lengthy) fiction in segments: in periodicals, as independent serial volumes, and as three-and four decker novels (which all depend for sales on creating a desire for more), *Silas Marner* stands out as an Eliot stand-alone novel of unusually manageable length. *Silas Marner's* comparative brevity seduces without addicting.

During the years I have been writing and teaching about "Literature and Intoxication" much jocularity has accompanied descriptions of my projects, jocularity divided about evenly between Eliot's reputation for ponderous sobriety on the one hand and my own motives in choice of topic on the other.

Despite the seriousness of Eliot's matter and tone, many scholars have emphasized the humour that surfaces throughout her novels, some of it precipitated by her addicted characters. In *Janet's Repentance* the narrator describes the aftermath of an anti-Evangelical meeting at the Red Lion: "Several friends of sound religion were conveyed home with some difficulty, one of them showing a dogged determination to seat himself in the gutter" (*Scenes of Clerical Life* NY: Penguin 1972, 283).

In *Middlemarch*, the narrator observes of the alcoholic Raffles: "To say that Mr. Raffles' manner was rather excited would be only one mode of saying that it was evening" (Ch. 53, books.google.com.).

While Eliot's theory of addiction offers hope and consolation about an all-too-serious problem, she does not resist the temptation to make occasional fun of her stumbling drunks as well.

About the Contributor

Kathleen McCormack is Professor Emerita, Department of English, Florida International University. Her books include *George Eliot and Intoxication: Dangerous Drugs for the Condition of England* (2000, 2001), *George Eliot's English Travels: Composite Characters and Coded Communications* (2005), and *George Eliot in Society: Travels Abroad and Sundays at the Priory* (2013).

Chapter 13

But Why Always *Middlemarch?*
My favourite George Eliot book:
Adam Bede

Bob Muscutt

Given the current popularity of *Middlemarch*, the choice of *Adam Bede* as my favourite Eliot novel requires some justification. That's fine, as while trying to explain to others why I love and admire the book so much, maybe I will clarify those reasons for myself.

We know that, when publication began in January, 1859, *Adam Bede* enjoyed immediate success with the reading public, and that respected reviewers hailed it as the work of a top flight novelist. Eliot's publisher, the canny businessman and perceptive reader, John Blackwood, stuck his neck out and predicted high sales, but they actually exceeded even his expectations.

But what about today, in the two hundredth anniversary of the novelist's birth and 160 years after the first copies hit Mudie's circulating library?

Yes, the book deserves its reputation as the first great realist novel in English. Eliot scholars refer to articles she wrote for the *Westminster Review*, in particular *The Natural History of German Life*, as well as the (in)famous Chapter XVII of the novel itself, to validate this important claim.

But do we really think about this impact on the history of English literature when getting to grips with the novel?

I don't.

Put generally, two major features of the book appeal most strongly to me. Firstly, its choice of what we can call the social range covered by all the characters, whether major or minor. Think of the book as a painting – something Eliot herself did in the Chapter XVII already mentioned. All the characters in the picture contribute to the overall effect of the canvas. They incorporate the social range of the novel, from top to bottom, if I may use that phrase.

So, who is sitting on the top rung of this social ladder? Squire Donnithorne and the Rector Irwine, both below gentry. Arthur, Squire Donnithorne's nephew, eventually inherits the estate, but, for reasons which may spoil a first reading of the novel, becomes a professional soldier and almost dies from the rigours of war.

Let's descend, and see whom we meet on the way down.

The Poysers; Mr Poyser is in the third generation of successful tenant farmers, but his wife, the dynamic brains behind the successful family business, has a more proletarian background. And then, if we exclude Arthur, we encounter the first major character, the wonderful and beautiful Hetty Sorrel, the orphaned niece of Mr Poyser, working for the Poysers as a dairymaid and domestic servant, and dreaming of becoming a lady's maid. She has other aspirations too, but, again, they would be spoilers.

By the way, I say "wonderful" because in my opinion Hetty, almost against the Narrator's wishes, leaves the deepest footprint, both on the characters in the novel, and, in my case at least, on the modern reader. Apart from *Romola*, no full length Eliot novel bore a woman's name as its title. Along with *Daniel Deronda's* Gwendolen Harleth, I think Hetty deserved that honour.

Slightly below Hetty, we have the novel's eponymous hero, Adam Bede, and his misunderstood brother Seth, both artisans or journeymen, as are most of the male population of Hayslope, the fictional Staffordshire village where much of the book's action takes place. These artisans and tradesmen provide the equivalent to the milieu of *Middlemarch*, in which a young but well-born doctor and the upwardly mobile builder's family, the Garths, occupy the bottom rung.

We can, therefore, say that the highest rung in *Adam Bede* corresponds approximately to the lowest rung in *Middlemarch*. This, of course, doesn't make one or the other a better novel. But I am not trying to make that judgement.

Our descent continues to another major character, Dinah Morris, Mrs Poyser's niece, whose rough hands reveal her proletarian identity, a "working woman". In answer to Lisbeth Bede, Adam's mother, she says with neither pride nor shame:

"'I am Dinah Morris, and I work in the cotton mill when I am at home.'"

I love that sentence.

In the novel as a whole, Dinah's vocation as a revivalist Methodist preacher takes precedence over her daily work as a mill hand, a manual worker in one of the first factories of the industrial revolution, probably the Arkwright mill near Cromford. This striking statement of identity prompted Valentine Cunningham, a literary scholar and Methodist historian, to remark that this is an "I" worthy of our attention.

Dinah, in both her role as revivalist Methodist preacher and as mill hand, provides the brief but highly significant link to what we might call "the dark village", the cottagers and squatters, who barely manage to exist with the few and dwindling rights to use yet unenclosed common land they still have. Dinah reaches out, apparently at great personal risk, to the lead miners, whom she describes in the Biblical but eloquent phrase as "sheep without a shepherd".

This brings us to the second overall feature of the novel which makes it so appealing to me personally.

Two great English historians, Lord Acton and Asa Briggs, greatly admired George Eliot as a novelist, but they also acknowledged her gifts as a historian.

In his essay on *Middlemarch* (*The Collected Essays of Asa Briggs*, Vol 2) Briggs states quite categorically: "Eliot had the gifts of a historian." (51) But what impressed both Briggs and Lord Acton was not so much Eliot's knowledge of history, but her ability as a novelist to make it live in the characters and the drama of the book. I think this what Briggs meant when he wrote in the Preface to *The Collected Essays of Asa Briggs Volume One* that "It is a mistake ... to treat history as "background" and "literature" as text." As he points out, " . . history and literature deal with human experience, both common or individual ... " (xvii)

This fusion of the fictional drama with the real, historical past – most of the action of the novel takes place sixty years before its publication, and almost 20 years before Eliot's birthday - occurs many times in the novel. In fact, it saturates the novel.

Dinah's revivalist Methodism and its persistent efforts to make contact with the urban poor, conform very closely with the realities of revivalist Methodism and religious dissent in Derbyshire in 1800.

But I would like to illustrate Eliot's ability to let her characters speak and act as individuals in their historical setting with one of the most popular scenes in the book.

It stars Mrs Rachel Poyser, who was famously quoted in the House of Parliament soon after the book's appearance. The scene, Chapter XXXII Mrs Poyser 'Has Her Say Out', is often viewed as comedy, which it most certainly partly is, but it is also rooted in the economic realities in agriculture in the years of the Napoleonic wars, a very profitable time for arable farmers and landowners.

Cereals, much needed to feed the soldiers, unlike dairy and other perishable products, could be transported abroad, and commanded high prices.

At the risk of losing their tenancy, Mrs Poyser stands her ground when the detested Squire Donnithorne tries first to cajole and then to intimidate the Poysers into making what are for them very unfavourable changes to their agricultural production. He demands a shift of emphasis from arable to dairy products which, apart from covering their own needs for milk, butter, and cheese, could only be sold to a very local market. In fact, their only customer would have been the Squire himself. Mrs Poyser's arguments show clearly that, although she is from a non-farming background, it is she who is the brains behind the successful farm, and who sees through the landlord's plans and rejects them.

Squire Donnithorne threatens not to extend the Poysers' lease and to install Mr Thurle, "a man of some capital" in their place. He directs this threat at Mr Poyser, who, as Donnithorne expects, is "alarmed at the possibility of their leaving the old place where he had been born and bred", but it is Mrs Poyser who responds, again expressing in almost Biblical language the essential business reality of the situation.

She describes the dilapidated state of the farm caused by Donnithorne's stinginess and refusal to carry out necessary repairs, which are his duty as landlord, and then she sums this up:

"See if you'll get a stranger to lead such a life here as that.: a maggot must be born i' the rotten cheese to like it, I reckon."

At this point Donnithorne realizes he is a beaten man, and leaves without another word.

This is indeed a great comic scene, verbally and visually. But I want to emphasize that Mrs Poyser's insight, based on personal experience, agree exactly with economic and historical reality. The capitalisation of farming was indeed beginning in England in the late eighteenth century. Men like Thurle, attracted by the high profits guaranteed by government contracts at war-time prices, were investing surplus capital in agriculture.

While Donnithorne's threats are historically real, and dramatically convincing, both he and Mrs Poyser know that it would not be in his best interests to carry them out. It is interesting that it is Mrs Poyser who grasps the economic truth more clearly than her more subservient husband, and has the courage to express it.

Almost as if he were commenting on the Donnithorne-Poyser confrontation, another great historian Hobsbawm writes in *Captain Swing*, a study of social unrest in the early decades of the eighteenth century that " . . for various reasons the tenant almost certainly had rather the better of the deal with the landlord." He explains that "the farmer had the advantage of being indispensable" and that " . . efficient farmers were not easy to find." The Poysers, therefore, would not have to compete for the tenancy with " . . a queue of land-hungry peasants or small-holders ... ." (31) Mrs Poyser's assessment of the situation was therefore spot on.

This poses the question: Where did Eliot derive her knowledge of Derbyshire around the turn of the eighteenth century? Certainly it was gathered from systematic reading, but much gleaned verbally from her Aunt Elisabeth, the original for Dinah Morris, and her husband Samuel, who was the original for Seth Bede, Adam's somewhat problematical younger brother. Eliot's father, Robert Evans, who grew up in Ellastone, a village many say is the real Hayslope, told her about his early life in the area they visited together at least once. Eliot also admitted that she used details from her father's life and work in her portrayal of Adam Bede.

If, as I recently did, you visit that area around Wirksworth, Ellastone, and Cromford, as well as the nearby old lead mining sites, you may notice how the landscape still offers evidence of its association with the novel.

The excellent local museums reinforce this impression as do a number of local buildings – the house where Elisabeth and Samuel Evans lived in Wirksworth, for example, and a staggering number of Methodist, especially Primitive Methodist, chapels, most of which are no longer used for worship.

I felt this much more strongly than with other Midlands locations of Eliot's novels. And I say that as native of Nuneaton, where Eliot was also born 200 years ago as Mary Anne Evans!

To make these connections, you would, of course, have had to have read the novel. If you haven't read it, I hope very much that this short and very personal view of some aspects of the book may encourage you to do so.

Enjoy!

About the contributor

Bob Muscutt born in Nuneaton, studied in Exeter and Leicester, UK, and has lived in Germany for over 40 years. Primarily a George Eliot enthusiast and researcher, his interests cover the long nineteenth century, and he has had articles appear in the George Eliot Review and the George Eliot-George Henry Lewes Studies Journal.

In addition to a novel based on George Eliot, he has published a dramatisation as well as a factual account of the life, trial, and hanging of his great, great grandmother in Coventry in 1849. He has recently played a major role in creating a George-Eliot-in-Weimar blog as a contribution to the 2019 bicentenary celebrations.

Chapter 14

"Tulliver's Travels"
Adapting *The Mill on the Floss* for Young Audiences

Margaret D. Stetz

In 1980, A. S. Byatt began her essay titled "George Eliot: A Celebration" with remarks that were anything but celebratory.

Instead, she described reading *The Mill on the Floss* at age eleven and finding it "unbearable." The "inexorable damping-down of the fire and energy" of Maggie Tulliver, Eliot's heroine, had angered her. Maggie's eventual fate, moreover—"drowning *with her brother*"—had seemed to her utterly wrong, leaving her, "a child reader," feeling "cheated."[1]

Only a year earlier, in her Introduction for the 1979 Penguin Classics edition of *The Mill on the Floss*, Byatt had demonstrated that early impressions leave lasting effects. There, she produced a more sophisticated version of essentially the same judgment. When it came to Eliot's decision to conclude the novel with the Flood, echoes of an eleven-year-old's disappointment still rang in Byatt's mature critical voice. For her, the result wasn't tragedy, but "incoherence."

---

1. A. S. Byatt. "George Eliot: A Celebration." *Passions of the Mind: Selected Writings.* London: Chatto and Windus, 1991. 72.

Again, too, she complained of the author's over-attention to the unsatisfying sister-and-brother relationship, saying, "Maggie's powers and frustrations have less to do with Tom for us than for George Eliot."[2]

It is entirely possible that Byatt's adult objections would have been the same, had she never read the novel as a girl. Nonetheless, the clarity with which she recalled her intense resistance to it, and her wish to preserve and share that youthful feeling more than thirty years afterwards, suggests how important early encounters with this novel can be.

The Mill on the Floss, more than many Victorian works intended for adults that also find their way into the hands of young readers, may have a greater impact, because Eliot devotes so much time to the lives of the two Tulliver children. Such a focus invites identification, but also fury whenever the story moves in directions of which a young audience disapproves.

Given the potential of Eliot's novel to interest that audience—and also to reach parents and school librarians looking to purchase "classic" titles that represent prestige and cultural cachet—publishers have tried, across the decades, to produce editions of it that they think will be appealing to children. In numerous cases, this has meant adding illustrations. Sometimes, these are anachronistic ones, meant to shrink the distance between past and present, so that Tom and Maggie do not actually resemble nineteenth-century characters. Maggie, especially, turns up often, both in girlhood and adulthood, as a figure who just happens to be wearing a long dress, but appears otherwise modern.

---

2. A. S. Byatt. "Introduction." *The Mill on the Floss* by George Eliot. Ed. A. S. Byatt. London: Penguin, 1979. 38.

Making the strange seem familiar was no doubt the aim in placing a photo on the front cover of the 1999 *The Mill on the Floss* in the British "Penguin Readers" series (Pearson Education Ltd.). The photo is of two actors from Graham Theakston's 1997 BBC TV adaptation of the novel, which numerous U.K. and later U. S. viewers of all ages had watched.

Here, Maggie—who is wearing very un-Victorian makeup—embodies late-twentieth-century, not mid-nineteenth-century, beauty standards. Her appearance invites children to imagine a heroine who conforms to notions of feminine glamour with which they are already comfortable.

What the half-dozen late-twentieth and twenty-first-century editions that I have examined—all of them, including those out of print, readily available through either Amazon.co.uk or Amazon.com—have in common, beyond this intent to provide visual hooks for Eliot's text, is compression.

All share a belief, articulated by the dust-jacket copy for Collins's 1974 "Classics for Today" edition, that publishers should cater to short attention spans and busy lives: "the book is now a length that can be coped with by the child who has many other things to do with his or her leisure time." Reading is assumed to be merely one of a number of potential activities, rather than a major focus of attention; therefore, the experience must be abbreviated according to adults' ideas of what is manageable and appropriate.

A 2013 adaptation of Eliot's novel "Retold by Gill Tavner" comes with this dust-jacket announcement of the goal of "Real Reads" editions: "Pick up these great little versions of the world's greatest books, and you'll discover that Real Reads are a Real Treat."

Presumably, picking up the weightier *Mill of the Floss* itself would not be a treat, so this "retelling" is only 64 pages long. It is by no means the shortest. That distinction belongs to a 2016 version published in New Delhi by Rupa. Even with numerous illustrations, some of them full-page, it clocks in at a mere 33 pages.

How this shortening is accomplished varies. In some cases, it involves editing Eliot's own text through a process of deletion; individual words or whole episodes and chapters vanish. In most, however, it relies on a so-called "retelling": the substitution of someone else's language for Eliot's. This compression is also nothing new—nothing to attribute to any recent speeding up of the pace of life or shrinkage of leisure time. *Tom and Maggie Tulliver*—a 1909 adaptation in the "Golden River" series of Thomas Nelson and Sons (named for John Ruskin's *The King of the Golden River*)— begins with Mr. Tulliver's declaration that he wants to educate Tom and closes with Maggie's arrival at King's Lorton to bring her brother home from school: "And now that the great event had come, his school years seemed like a holiday that had come to an end" are the book's final words.[3] This latter sentence is a rewriting—a clumsy one, with repetition of the verb "come," unlike Eliot's more elegant original: "And now his school years seemed like a holiday that had come to an end."

More important, gone is the memorable conclusion to Book Second—the lyrical commentary of Eliot's narrator: "They had entered the thorny wilderness, and

---

3. [Anon.] Tom and Maggie Tulliver. Told from George Eliot's 'The Mill on the Floss'. London: Thomas Nelson and Sons, 1909. 155.

the golden gates of their childhood had for ever closed behind them,"[4]

Indeed, gone in general is the first-person narrator. In many of these abridgements—including the 1992 "Penguin Readers" edition; the 2013 "Real Reads" edition; and the 2016 "Red Turtle Junior Classics" edition—there is no sign of Chapter One, "Outside Dorlcote Mill," where the narrative as a whole is framed as the speaker's recollection. Various adapters have decided that children could never be drawn into a tale that opens with an adult's memories and musings.

Equally interesting are two other patterns of deletion, involving content that appears to have been regarded as inflammatory or otherwise unsuitable for young audiences. As an eleven-year-old feminist *avant la lettre*, A. S. Byatt had revolted against the "damping-down of the fire and energy" of Maggie Tulliver. For other girl readers, too, a sense of outrage begins with this assessment by Maggie's father, in Eliot's Chapter Two: "'The little 'un takes after my side, now; she's twice as 'cute as Tom. Too 'cute for a woman, I'm afraid'. . . 'It's no mischief much while she's a little 'un, but an over 'cute woman's no better nor a long-tailed sheep—she'll fetch none the bigger price for that.'"[5]

His second set of remarks, likening women to livestock in the marketplace, is absent from nearly every version of the novel designed for children.

Publishers' fears not only of offending potential book buyers, of whatever age, but of mis-educating impressionable audiences, seem to be the driving force

---

4.   [4] George Eliot, *The Mill on the Floss*. Ed. A. S. Byatt. London: Penguin, 1979. 270.

5.   George Eliot, *The Mill on the Floss*. Ed. A. S. Byatt. London: Penguin, 1979. 59-60

behind omissions of another controversial feature of Eliot's text: its racist depiction of Romani people in Chapter Eleven, "Maggie Tries to Run Away from her Shadow."

This episode, which instils both in Maggie herself and in readers a sense of unease about the inhabitants of a so-called "gypsy" camp, along with the belief that they are thieves who steal from naïve English children, is entirely missing from, for instance, the 2017 Rupa Publications adaptation. More significant, however, is the manner of rewriting this cross-cultural incident in Oxford University Press's 2007 *The Mill on the Floss* in its "Oxford Progressive English Readers" series.

In this version, "Retold by Rosemary Border," Maggie still runs away from home after pushing her cousin Lucy Dean into the mud. What follows, though, is markedly different: "Meanwhile Maggie only got as far as the next village. There she met a kind old man, who took her home."[6]

Is it worse to reaffirm xenophobic prejudices and suggest that the motives of adults who are strangers should be viewed with suspicion, or to proffer the myth of a "kind old man"—presumably, a white Englishman—whom little girls supposedly can trust to bring them home safely?

Which is the more dangerous lesson?

Here, it may be difficult to choose—as well as to see how this flatfooted intervention fits with the avowed aims of this Oxford series: "to intrigue, mystify, amuse, delight and stimulate the imagination."

---

6. Rosemary Border. *The Mill on the Floss* by George Eliot. Retold by Rosemary Border. Second Edition. Oxford: Oxford University Press, 2007. 14

Surely the most distressing features of these adaptations, however, are the short author biographies that accompany them. To anyone who cares about sparking interest in earlier women writers in general, or in George Eliot in particular, these potted "lives" are a disaster. Again and again, they silence and censor Eliot's romantic, sexual, and domestic conduct. All the information that the 2013 "Real Reads" volume, for instance, provides is that "George Eliot" was a woman's pseudonym, that *The Mill on the Floss* was her second novel, and that she wrote philosophy before turning to fiction. After this comes nothing but a brief discussion of themes in the novel.

Worse still is the Introduction to Rosemary Border's "retelling" for the 2007 second edition of Oxford's *The Mill on the Floss*, which informs readers that Mary Anne Evans had "an older brother who was important to her." It continues: "They were happy when they were young. Later, though, Evans did something her brother hated. He was very angry, and said she was not respectable."[7]

What is this nameless "something" so unspeakable that children cannot be told about it? Will they connect the puzzling word "respectable"—which may be meaningful in a Victorian context, but not necessarily in a modern one—with anything that might make sense to them? And will George Eliot's personal history help to promote the notion of a woman's right to her own desires and sexuality, which is a valuable lesson for readers at every age?

That seems unlikely.

---

7. Rosemary Border. *The Mill on the Floss* by George Eliot. Retold by Rosemary Border. Second Edition. Oxford: Oxford University Press, 2007. vi

Perhaps surprisingly, the boldest biographical summary occurs in 1974, in an "Editor's Note" for the Collins version. It not only reports that Eliot "lived very happily" with George Henry Lewes "as man and wife until his death," but that she later married "John Cross, twenty years her junior," and it points out the implicit hypocrisy: "Her brother Isaac broke his long silence and sent her a letter of congratulation. She was respectable at last in the eyes of Victorian society!" On the other hand, while stating that "she was never able to marry Lewes," it refuses to say explicitly what prevented her.[8] Nor does this short biography—or any other, in these volumes for young readers—ever apply the word "feminist" to George Eliot or mention the existence of her circle of equally intellectual and socially radical women friends, although such information could prove inspiring, especially to girls.

Judging by adaptations such as these, the Tullivers have not fared well in their travels across decades, borders, and audiences.

Neither has George Eliot herself.

While I would like to think that some abridgements and "retellings" of *The Mill on the Floss* have resulted in happier experiences for young readers than A. S. Byatt had at age eleven, I have my doubts.

Mostly, I am glad that I waited to read the novel, in its uncondensed and uncensored form, until I was an undergraduate—old enough to confront its problematic attitudes, but also to appreciate the matchless poetry of its original language and its ageless wisdom. Although

8. [Anon.] "Editor's Note." *The Mill on the Floss* by George Eliot. "Classics for Today" edition. London: William Collins & Sons, 1974. 6

it was *Middlemarch* that Virginia Woolf famously honoured with the label of a novel "for grown-up people," *The Mill on the Floss*, too, deserves that status. Its opening sections may focus on children, but it offers compelling pictures of childhood that only adults can fully appreciate, because only adults can recognize and understand the social systems—the sexism, the class hierarchies, and indeed the racism—that determine the reactions both of and to Eliot's characters and limit their lives.

Eliot reveals these operations, moreover, with a sly and sometimes openly satirical humour that cuts in many directions, including back at readers and their own world. That we have not yet made ours a better one—that dark, smart, rebellious girls and women like Maggie continue to feel like outcasts, while images of blonde, white, irritatingly doll-like Lucy Deans populate millions of websites as the ideal—is one more reason why *The Mill on the Floss* needs to be read now by those with the power to change the world.

About the Contributor

Margaret D Stetz Margaret D. Stetz is the Mae and Robert Carter Professor of Women's Studies and Professor of Humanities at the University of Delaware, USA. Previously, she had taught at the University of Virginia and Georgetown University. As well as being author of books such as *British Women's Comic Fiction, 1890-1990* and *Facing the Late Victorians*— and co-editor (with Bonnie B. C. Oh) of *Legacies of the Comfort Women of WWII* and of *Michael Field and Their World* (with Cheryl A. Wilson) —she has published over 120 essays and chapters in journals and edited collections on topics ranging from Victorian feminism, to the politics of animated films, to fashion and authorship, to wartime sexual violence. She has been curator or co-curator (with Mark Samuels Lasner) of more than a dozen exhibitions on turn-of-the-century gender, art, literature, book history, and print culture, including "Everything Is Going on Brilliantly: Oscar Wilde and Philadelphia" at the Rosenbach of the Free Library of Philadelphia in Spring 2015 and "Richard Le Gallienne, Liverpool's Wild(e) Poet" at Liverpool Central Library (UK) in 2016, with an upcoming exhibition on Max Beerbohm and celebrity caricature scheduled for 2021 in New York City. She has also co-organized numerous symposia and conferences, such as the first international academic conference in the U.S. on Japanese WWII military sexual slavery (in 1996). In 2015, she was named by *Diverse: Issues in Higher Education* magazine to its list of the top 25 women in higher education

Chapter 15

My Pleasure Reading George Eliot's Novels

Shinsuke Hori

The literary fame of Eliot has now spread over the world and it is echoed in Japan, a distant country from England. Reading Eliot teaches us the pleasure of reading literature. In Japanese, *bungaku* means literature; *bun* signifies words and *gaku* signifies learning. In other words, when we read the works of *bungaku,* we are supposed to learn and pursue the meaning and essence of words.

I think that there is no other author than Eliot where we can feel the importance and pleasure of learning words. When we read her works, we have to remind ourselves that missing the profound meaning of a single word is actually missing the pleasure of reading *bungaku.*

In this sense, Eliot embodies the pleasure of reading *bungaku.*

She looks at the heart of a thing and describes it with truthful details. Her eyes looking at the world are moral and philosophical. Her ideas are complicatedly woven into the text, but they permit us a diversity of reading. Like in a well-known phrase in *Middlemarch*, "Signs are small measurable things, but interpretations are illimitable" (Book I Chap. 2 23).

Every single word Eliot uses has a profound significance in the text and encourages us to search for its meaning among illimitable interpretations.

We enjoy reading Eliot for this illimitability.

> A wide plain, where the broadening Floss hurries on between its green banks to the sea, and the loving tide, rushing to meet it, checks its passage with an impetuous embrace.
> (The Mill on the Floss Book 1 Chap. 1 7)

I still remember the feelings I felt when I read *The Mill on the Floss* for the first time. That was when I was doing a Masters course in the UK, and I couldn't put the novel down.

It was difficult for me to read because I had just started reading Victorian fiction then. However, soon after I started reading it, I noticed Eliot's illuminating love of nature especially found in the opening scene.

Eliot's nature has a sympathetic tone resounding with humanely kindness. For me, it is more than real, and makes me feel as if I were actually part of the scene. While I was reading the passage, I felt every sentence and word combining together to create vivid picture images in my mind.

After the reading experience of *The Mill on the Floss*, I began to seek the roots of this love of nature in Eliot's writing. It never goes wrong and always remains calm. It is touchingly delicate. The nature she depicts is produced by her detailed observation of it.

> Nature has her language, and she is not unveracious; but we don't know all the intricacies of her syntax just yet, and in a hasty reading we may happen to extract the very opposite of her real meaning.
> (*Adam Bede* Chapter 15 139)

Eliot's language of nature has its own intricate syntax, but it is also a proof of her truthful attitude to it. She puts the richness of feelings into the descriptions of natural landscape. I knew through reading Eliot that nature conveyed human feelings of sadness, happiness, desperation, and expectation. Hetty Sorrel's desperate journey in search of Arthur Donnithorne is filled with descriptions of nature which tell of the delicate vicissitudes of human feelings.

I often felt confused when I came across Eliot's descriptions of nature extending over a page without ending with a period. However, Eliot's words, full of her philosophical and religious ideas, drew me into the pleasure of reading. Every word of Eliot required me to read on and look deeply into the meaning of it.

I especially felt pleasure in reading about nature. It is not necessarily that simple to feel sympathy with her depiction of it. Eliot depicts the natural landscape in a way that we feel as if it is actually before our eyes.

The natural landscape reflecting Hetty Sorrel's desperation is real because Eliot depicts it in a way that we feel sympathy with it. This is why we share Eliot's love of nature.

> She tried to have hope and trust, though it was hard to believe that the future would be anything else than the harvest of the seed that was being sown before her eyes. But always there is seed being sown silently and unseen, and everywhere there come sweet flowers without our foresight or labour. We reap what we sow, but Nature has love over and above that justice, and gives us shadow and blossom and fruit that spring from no planting of ours.
>
> (*Janet's Repentance* 204)

The seeds of human motives later bloom into flowers and become the vehicles of human feelings. Janet Dempster in *Janet's Repentance* cannot see where the seeds of her unhappiness were sown.

We have sympathy for the misfortunes of Eliot's characters; Janet, Hetty and Maggie's failure to see a natural process of how a tiny seed later comes to bloom into flowers. A seed is a natural and moral object driving Eliot's impulse of sympathy.

> In hilly districts, where houses and clusters of houses look so tiny against the huge limbs of Mother Earth one cannot help thinking of man as a parasitical animal—an epizoon making his abode on the skin of the planetary organism.
> (Recollections of Weimar 1854 265)

> Besides, a man with the milk of human kindness in him can scarcely abstain from doing a good-natured action, and one cannot be good-natured all round. Nature herself occasionally quarters an inconvenient parasite on an animal towards whom she has otherwise no ill-will. What then? We admire her care for the parasite.
> (*The Mill on the Floss* Book I Chap. 3 27)

The more I read Eliot, the more I came to know about her love of nature.

My current research interest is "Recollections" of her European and British travels from 1854 to 1860. When I first read them, my first impression was Eliot's delight with nature and her delightful sense of natural space. She is a naturalist, observing the natural world with a naturalist's eyes. She looks at the heart of a natural object and finds the roots of human motives from the observation.

They are also full of her sympathetic tones. Eliot's sympathy is not only in her descriptions of nature, but also in their story-like construction. Every figure she meets during travels looks like her fictional characters: Janet, Hetty, and Maggie. We can feel sympathy with their life.

Every time I read Eliot, every time I find something new. It is probably not enough to say that Eliot's descriptions of nature are vivid and real. She loves nature and we feel her love of it. How many times more will I read Eliot?

How many new things will I find by reading her? I feel like I cannot still understand even the half of Eliot's love of nature.

I will continue reading her for this.

References

Eliot, George.

   Adam Bede. Oxford: Oxford UP, 2008.
   Middlemarch. Oxford, New York: Oxford UP, 2008.
   The Mill on the Floss. Oxford: Oxford UP, 1996.
   Scenes of Clerical Life. Oxford: Oxford UP, 2015.

Harris, Margaret, and Judith Johnston, eds. *The Journals of George Eliot.* Cambridge: Cambridge UP, 1998.

About the contributor

Shinsuke Hori did a Masters course at the University of Sussex. He is currently a part-time lecturer of English at Nihon University in Japan. His most recent article is 'George Eliot's Three "Recollections" and Romola: Her Realistic Programme, Visual Perception of the Natural, Social, and Historical World, and Proto-fiction' (*The George Eliot Review of Japan* 2017.

Part 4

Her Beautiful Mind

Worlds of Thought, Within and Beyond the Books

Chapter 16

George Eliot and Brexit

Dr Catherine Brown

In Eliot's last complete novel she tried out lots of things for the first time. For example, she set the story in the near present (the novel was written 1874-6 and set in the 1860s), whereas most of her fictions are set around three decades before the time of writing.

This up-to-dateness fits with *Daniel Deronda* being the most avant-garde and forward-thinking of her works. It came out more than a decade before Freud's major writings started appearing, but in this book more than in anything else she wrote, Eliot explored the unconscious. *Daniel Deronda* has a psychological depth which inspired Henry James (particularly *Portrait of a Lady*, 1881) and D.H. Lawrence (particularly *Women in Love*, 1919).

But – you might respond – what about Grandcourt?

Whereas Eliot's other bad characters – Dunstan Cass in *Silas Marner*, Tito Melema in *Romola*, Nicholas Bulstrode and John Raffles in *Middlemarch* – are a mixture of good and evil, and might in other circumstances have found happiness, in Henleigh Mallinger Grandcourt Eliot creates her first honest-to-goodness villain. Unlike the others he enjoys giving pain, and his badness in combination with his aristocracy (another first for this novel is that Eliot moves beyond depicting artisans, farmers, the middle classes and minor gentry to representing the high aristocracy) gives him the aspect of a stereotypical, even stage, villain.

But the profundity comes in how his minor actions point to the major actions that we do not see, because they unconsciously express the same impulses.

Take, for example, the moment when Grandcourt tells his new wife Gwendolen to put on diamonds for dinner.

As he suspects, she has a horror of these jewels, because they were sent to her on her wedding day with a curse from his former lover. (Before her family was financially ruined, Gwendolen had promised this woman that she would never marry Grandcourt). At first Gwendolen hesitates, but:

> That white hand of his which was touching his whisker was capable, she fancied, of clinging round her neck and threatening to throttle her ...
> 'Oblige me by telling me your reason for not wearing the diamonds when I desire it,' said Grandcourt. His eyes were still fixed upon her, and she felt her own eyes narrowing under them as if to shut out an entering pain. 'He delights in making the dogs and horses quail: that is half his pleasure in calling them his,' she said to herself
> 'You want some one to fasten them,' he said, coming toward her.
> She did not answer, but simply stood still, leaving him to take out the ornaments and fasten them as he would . . . Grandcourt inwardly observed that she answered to the rein.

This passage tells us as much about this couple's sex life as we ever learn, but it is enough, and contains much that could never be said explicitly in a Victorian novel. It strongly hints that Gwendolen experiences sex as 'an entering pain', to which she submits only out of fear of still greater violence, and which it is Grandcourt's pleasure to inflict.

Since he rides her like a horse, he may also beat her as he beats his horses. By the same token, his sadism towards animals may have a sexual dimension. Here we are in darker psychological territory than any that Eliot had entered before.

But Grandcourt is not an isolated moral monster; he is just the worst extreme of an aristocracy, and more generally an England, which is presented as corrupt, lifeless (Grandcourt only really comes alive when he's inflicting pain), and desperately in need of renewal.

Several of the novel's families have only girl children, suggesting – two decades after Darwin's *The Origin of Species* started raising questions about human survival – that English society does not even have the means of continuing itself.

Many of the characters are complacent and chauvinist – ignorant about the rest of the world, but convinced that England is better than it.

What's the solution?

Throwing open the novel, the titular hero's mind, and the hero's life, to that world. I cannot think of a single Victorian novel which weighs in more strongly on 'Remain' side of the Brexit debate than does *Daniel Deronda*.

The hero Daniel quits Cambridge University because he wants to avoid 'a merely English attitude in studies'

(DD: 155). Oxbridge education at that time concentrated on the Classics and mathematics, and largely ignored modern Europe thought. As George Eliot (who translated German into English) knew – and as the failed scholar Casaubon in *Middlemarch* crucially does not know – much of the best work going on at the time in philosophy, archaeology, anthropology, linguistics, and history was happening in Germany, which is where Daniel travels to on leaving Cambridge.

Mordecai, the novel's visionary, 'went to Hamburg to study, and afterwards to Göttingen' (DD: 426).

Germany also produced Goethe, of whom Eliot's partner George Henry Lewes wrote a biography, and whose conception of *Weltliteratur* (literature that mediates between the world's countries and cultures) underlies the novel's willed and weighty internationalism.

For example: each chapter starts with a quotation. Some of these epigraphs are written by Eliot, but of those which are not, nearly half were originally written in (one of seven different) languages other than English.

When Eliot quotes French, German or Italian in the original, she does not (unlike modern editions) give translations, with the implicit message that if her readers do not already know these languages, then they should certainly start learning them (and, like all the novel's best characters, become multilingual).

Daniel Deronda's mother, as Daniel discovers part way through the novel, is an Italian Jew who had a career as a singer touring throughout Europe. The model for this character was Eliot's friend, the French Italian mezzo-soprano Pauline Viardot, who was as widely travelled as Alcharisi.

Eliot herself researched her novel by travelling to Bad Homberg, Frankfurt, Mainz, and Amsterdam. No passports were then needed to travel in Europe, and Eliot would have warmly welcomed the idea of the Schengen zone, which in 1995 made passport-free travel between most European countries possible again.

She would as certainly have deplored her home country cutting itself off from the easy travel, free health insurance, and possibility of working abroad, that are guaranteed by the European Union.

But the novel's internationalism extends well beyond the current boundaries of the EU. Viardot spent three years attached to the opera in St Petersburg, where the Russian novelist Turgenev fell in love with her.

Non-coincidentally, Deronda's mother ends up married to a Russian nobleman.

Eliot never shared the anti-Russian jingoism of her (and our) time; during the Crimean and Russo-Turkish wars she simply expressed sympathy for both sides. She also appreciated how popular her writings were in Russia.

Most of her novels came out in Russian within a year of their English publication, and *Adam Bede* went through three Russian editions in 1859 alone.

Daniel Deronda's gifted musician Klesmer, who shows up his English employers as both classist and racist, is 'a felicitous combination of the German, the Sclave and the Semite' (DD 206).

Which brings us to one of the most extraordinary aspects of the novel: its philo-Semitism.

Eliot lived in a time and place of mild active, and pervasive passive, anti-Semitism, and of profound ignorance as to what modern (as opposed to Biblical)

Judaism involved. Her hero Daniel starts out, as the reader is also assumed to do, with the standard level of ignorance. But as he gets mixed up with a Jewish girl, discovers that he himself is Jewish, and finally decides to dedicate himself to creating a home for his people in Palestine. His own knowledge of Judaism, and that of his readers, increase in tandem.

Eliot did a huge amount of research in order to get all this right, including learning Hebrew from a friend who worked at the British Museum. Emanuel Deutsch, the major model for Mordecai, died on his second trip to Palestine in 1873.

Not surprisingly, the novel was welcomed in Hebrew and Russian translations by East European Jews; and by the time that Israel was established in 1948, its three largest cities – Jerusalem, Tel Aviv and Haifa – had streets named after George Eliot in gratitude.

Certainly, the novel is named for its Jewish hero. Yet actually he occupies well under half the book. This points to the novel's biggest puzzle. What, ultimately, *is* the relationship between the novel's Gentile part (which focuses on Gwendolen and Grandcourt), and its Jewish part (which focuses on Daniel, his future wife Mirah, and her prophetic brother Mordecai)?

Most of the Gentile characters never meet most of the Jewish characters. Gwendolen has heard of Mordecai but shows no interest in him; he never learns of her existence. The two sets of characters are even described by a different narrative voice. The narrator of the Gentile story is dryly witty and satiric; the narrator of the Jewish story is earnest and idealistic, rather like Daniel himself. Gwendolen's story is all but a tragedy; Daniel's is in the end not just a personal romantic comedy, but gestures towards future triumphs for his people.

They're so different, no wonder many readers have favoured one half over the other. The critic F.R. Leavis famously (or notoriously) said that the 'questionably-emotional' Jewish half of the novel should be dumped and the novel renamed *Gwendolen Harleth* (*The Great Tradition* (1948), p. 84).

Early Hebrew and Russian translations of the novel, by contrast, ignored the Gentile half and presented only the Jewish story.

Eliot herself said that 'I meant everything in the book to be related to everything else there' (*The George Eliot Letters (1871-1881)*, ed. Gordon S. Haight, 9 vols. (1954-1978), vi, 290). Especially over the last fifty years, many critics have found that she was actually successful in making the two parts connected.

But I'm not so sure.

For all that Mordecai's understanding of the Jewish purpose is that it should mediate between nations, the novel itself doesn't operate a Schengen zone between its Gentile and Jewish worlds. Daniel can move from the former to the latter, but Gwendolen not only can't follow him, but has no equivalent place to escape to.

This creates a jarring contrast at the novel's end. She ends up in widowhood and distress, whilst Daniel's wedding is described in the most ideal terms.

Eliot had explored this dynamic before.

At the end of *Adam Bede*, the woman that Adam first loved, Hetty, dies in misery on her way to exile in Australia, whilst Adam gets married to his new love, Dinah.

On the one hand this divergence between fates is realistic. Life brings overwhelming pain, and phenomenal happiness, to different people, who may know each other, at the same time. But when a novel shows this, it has to make a moral negotiation, or be seen to fail to do so.

In Adam's case, his happiness in marriage is forever shadowed by his mourning for Hetty. Daniel's marriage doesn't seem to have this dimension, precisely because he *is* entering another world. In moral terms it is as though he, having jumped ship from a corrupt and limited England to a world of idealism, deserves the unalloyed happiness that comes with it – whereas Gwendolen suffers as a kind of scapegoat for the corruption and limitations that define her world.

This isn't fair, but it is an indicator of the rage that Eliot felt, at this late stage in her life, at her country's provincialism, complacency, arrogance, racism, and the declining education levels of its elites.

Where, we might ask, was Eliot going next?

Her next book *Impressions of Theophrastus Such* (1879) also indicates the increasing breath of her social range, increasing innovation in form, greater passion in critique, and greater radicalism of proposed solutions.

George Eliot the 'realist' had by the time that she died aged sixty-one embraced the functions of a prophet – both in foretelling the future (in this case, Israel's creation), and in criticising her own society. It is our and the world's loss that she could not continue the developments of her strange and great late phase – but she did leave us with a novel which you may well find resonates with the turbulent, end-of-empire feel of our age.

About the Contributor

Catherine Brown BA (Cantab), MSc (Lond), MA (Lond), PhD (Cantab) studied English at Cambridge, then politics and comparative literature in London, before returning to Cambridge for her PhD as an English-Russian comparatist. She has taught post 1800 literature at the universities of Cambridge, Greenwich, and Oxford, and in September 2012 joined New College of the Humanities in London as Head of English and Senior Lecturer in English literature.

Catherine is the author of the monograph *The Art of Comparison: How Novels and Critics Compare* (Legenda, 2011), and articles on George Eliot, D.H. Lawrence, Henry James, and Lev Tolstoy – and co-editor of *The Reception of George Eliot in Europe* (Bloomsbury, 2015).

She is co-editor of the forthcoming *The Edinburgh Companion to DH Lawrence and the Arts* (forthcoming EUP 2020), and is Vice-President of the DH Lawrence Society of the UK. She tweets on matters sometimes related to D.H. Lawrence as: @NeoLawrencian.

Chapter 17

"The only novel Father has ever read!":
Vernon Lushington and *Adam Bede.*

David Taylor

If Susan Lushington's statement about her father's limited capacity for reading novels is correct, why did he, a lawyer and man of letters, choose *Adam Bede* to the exclusion of all the other great writers of the nineteenth century?

But why did Lushington's daughter, Susan, believe that *Adam Bede* was the only novel that her father had read? What was it about this novel in particular that might have appealed to him so much?

Vernon Lushington (1832-1912) has, for many years, been a shadowy figure in the lives of many of the great artists, writers and musicians of the nineteenth century. Until my discovery of the Lushington family archive he was usually, and quite unfairly, demoted to a mere footnote in the biographies of his well-known friends.

Lushington's family were firmly rooted within the "Intellectual Aristocracy" of Victorian England. Vernon had a remarkable circle of friends that included members of the Pre-Raphaelite Brotherhood; the writers Elizabeth Gaskell, George Gissing and Thomas Hardy; and the musicians Arthur Sullivan, Hubert Parry and Ralph Vaughan Williams. He was also one of the earliest British admirers of Walt Whitman and is credited as being amongst those who introduced the American's work to the British public. But, above all else, he was a disciple of Auguste Comte and a leading member of the London Positivist Society.

Attention is drawn to Lushington's relationship with Eliot when, in December 1880, among the large crowds gathered in the falling rain in London's Highgate Cemetery to catch a glimpse of the writer's funeral cortege, he is listed as being among the small, select group of those who had been "specially invited." Two years earlier, when Eliot's partner, G.H. Lewis was laid to rest, and "only a few old and intimate friends of the deceased" were present, standing with the literary giants Robert Browning and Anthony Trollope was the mysterious Lushington.

Frustratingly there is little in the archive that furthers our knowledge of Lushington's relationship with Eliot and we must look elsewhere for that. What we do know is restricted largely to a few of Eliot's published letters which reveal that Lushington's wife, a talented pianist, was a visitor at The Priory.

In May 1877 Eliot wrote that Jane was to pay a call to accompany the violinist Henry Holmes, another man associated with the London Positivist group. It was Holmes who had set Eliot's *The Choir Invisible* to music for performance at Newton Hall, the Positivists' meeting place on "The Day of the Dead" in 1883.

This annual commemoration, on the last day of the year, was a result of the Positivists refuting the Christian idea of a life after death. Instead they chose to believe that the departed lived on in the minds of others. The opening lines of Eliot's poem supports this idea.

O May I join the choir invisible
Of those immortal dead who live again
In minds made better by their presence: live
In pulses stirr'd to generosity,
In deeds of daring rectitude, in scorn
For miserable aims that end with self,
In thoughts sublime that pierce the night like
stars,
And with their mild persistence urge man's
search
To vaster issues.

Lushington later echoed Eliot's words in some verses of his own:

For in the Choir Invisible
The loved ones sing:
Still they love here, still with us dwell,
And blessing bring.

In 1877 an anonymous essayist had written that "George Eliot's world is the Comtist's world." Despite acknowledging that they had no biographical information to link Eliot to the followers of Comte, the writer still believed that they could discern the influence of Comte in her writing through the absence of Christian motives and concerns in her characters.

Eliot had been familiar with Comte's Positivism since the early 1850s. In 1859 she had met Richard Congreve who had inaugurated the Positivist movement in England. He in turn introduced her to three of his closest Positivist friends, John Henry Bridges, Frederic Harrison and Edward Spencer Beesly.

It was the Positivist movement that brought Lushington and Eliot together. Lushington was an ardent disciple of Auguste Comte and an enthusiastic evangelist of the bizarre Religion of Humanity. He regularly attended the London Positivist group meetings where he often spoke on areas in which he had a particular interest, especially the arts.

Frederic Harrison wrote that Eliot's death was a profound loss to the movement, though he acknowledged that she been only a partial believer. The publisher Charles Kegan Paul recalled how Eliot had written of Comte, "I will not submit to him my heart and my intellect." Another former Positivist sympathiser wrote that her novels offered only "refined morality, in general harmony with that of Auguste Comte."

In 1876 Eliot had herself written that her writing was "simply a set of experiments in life". In *The Natural History of German Life*, Eliot suggests that the purpose of literature is to expand readers' moral sympathies and imaginations. She believed that ethics and aesthetics were inseparable. Oscar Wilde wrote of Eliot that "she is the embodiment of philosophy in fiction."

Eliot rejected her early, simple, evangelical faith at a young age on moral and intellectual grounds. She was deeply influenced by Strauss's "Life of Jesus" and Feuerbach's "Essence of Christianity" both of which she translated in the 1840s and 50s. Eliot famously exclaimed, "God, immortality, duty - how inconceivable the first, how unbelievable the second, how peremptory and absolute the third."

Kathryn Hughes has commented that Eliot had "made a career – a great one – by creating a moral universe in her novels in which goodness was not dependent on belief in God. Instead, acts of kindness towards other people and an endurance of the pain and suffering that everyday life brings were, for her, the real spiritual teachers."

The answer to my original question about why would Lushington have elected *Adam Bede* is that at the heart of Comte's Religion of Humanity, lay the ideal of Altruism. *Adam Bede* is claimed to be a positivist allegory in which "Eliot portrays Dinah Morris as the pure embodiment of nature's altruistic moral order – so pure that she can serve as a reference point for the moral development of Adam himself." The novel contends not only that social order depends on altruism, but also that the germ of altruism lies in human nature itself. It was this altruism that led Vernon Lushington to declare to his bride to be on the eve of their wedding:

> Henceforth we will walk together in newness of life, in singleness of mind, striving to fulfil to the <u>uttermost</u> our duties to one another, to our dear relations & friends, and to that larger world, who whether rich or poor, <u>are</u> our brothers & sisters. Dearest Jane! I look to you truthfully, that you cherish me the highest, the widest purposes that I may have or shall have. Don't suffer me to make an idol of home-comfort, or professional eminence, or even of yourself, my precious one! Of me too it is required, as it is required of every one that I should give my Life for others.

Lushington had inherited a sense of public duty akin to altruism from his father and other family members. Like Eliot, any loss of traditional faith that he had experienced (his father being an ecclesiastical judge who counted himself within the fold of the Anglican broad-church movement) did not destroy the inherent desire of service to mankind and, perhaps, in some ways it only highlighted it.

Henry Sidgwick wrote, "The strongest conviction I have is what Comte called altruisme: the cardinal doctrine, it seems to me, of Jesus of Nazareth." Beatrice Webb believed altruism to be "the impulse of self-subordinating service" which, in the mid-nineteenth century, "was transformed, consciously and overtly from God to man".

Comte's altruism was considered quite different from anything similar which could be found within Christianity. The Positivists believed that their version of altruism was morally superior. Any form of self-sacrifice expressed with the Christian faith was flawed. It was essentially a selfish system because it was based on each individual's desire for reward at the end of life and fear of eternal punishment. Lushington's letter to his wife-to-be epitomises in him the essence of altruism.

Curiously, within the Lushington marriage in which Jane remained a devoutly committed Christian, there is a hint of the tensions that are found in the relationship of Dorothea and Casaubon in *Middlemarch*. This is revealed in another letter Jane wrote to her husband about an imaginary conversation she had had with him.

> I talked to you all the way & imagined sweet answers & shall I confess- some little seeing – or trying to see – with my eyes! & I tried to turn a deaf ear to the words "I am going one way & you another." Vernon, Dearest, am I not your wife – haven't I right to be gloried in – to work with you – rest with you - & highest pleasure of all – to soar with you. This was always my idea of a wife's happiness & if I know nothing of the world you go into – will you never help me go there.

Jane, like Dorothea, desperately longed for self-development and self-expression, for access to sources of profound and effectual knowledge, so that she could also share the privilege of contributing to the progress of humanity.

Susan's claim that *Adam Bede* was the only novel that her father had ever read was almost certainly wrong. For one thing her father had been a close friend of Elizabeth Gaskell, her "Cousin V", and who kept a room especially for him in her Manchester home whenever he was there on legal business.

Can we really believe that he had never read Gaskell's *Mary Barton*? This book epitomised so much of the Christian Socialistic ethic with which Lushington was deeply involved before it was replaced by Comte and Positivism.

Here in full are the two entries in Susan Lushington's 1894 diary from which the title of this article is taken:

> In the evening Uncle Godfrey read us some bits from Adam Bede. How different it is to any of the modern novels – George Meredith-Kipling – or even Stephenson – who all give you all the events – coming plump upon you like they do in real life - & not led up to & described beforehand almost as it were – which George Eliot does. I liked it enormously and found it extraordinarily sympathetic [and] real ... I should want to read a lot more before I got into it.

But just two days later she wrote:

> I sat up late last night reading Adam Bede – but I don't believe I care for it at all. Adam & Dinah are two medieval saints – who would never have existed in real life & if they had, they would have been bores or prigs! (This is great sacrilege & I feel I ought

scarcely to whisper it – even to you!) Hetty & Arthur are not well done either - & they all lack Humanity – except perhaps the Poysers - & the village people. I believe I should prefer it, if it were more of an essay – without attempting story & a plot - like her moralizings & little bits of philosophy if only they wouldn't interrupt almost every sentence in the conversation. It is curious to think that it is the only novel Father has ever read! It certainly has a wonderful sympathy of its own – only to me, it doesn't seem to fit into the story which it tells.

Despite having been "catechised" in Positivism from early age by her father, Susan sees Adam and Dinah in quite a different light to that which her father might have viewed them. They are "plaster saints" and "bores and prigs". This is in contrast to Dinah, one of the most altruistic of all Eliot's characters, being seen as Comte's exemplar. Comte believed that because women had smaller brains, they were intellectually inferior, but morally superior, to men. In the Positivist meeting houses the focus was not on an altar or a crucifix, but on the image of a woman and a child.

Setting aside the truth of Susan's statement about her father's restricted reading of novels, his obsession with Positivism led him to look for signs of it everywhere, even in the lives and writings of those who would not claim to accept Comte's philosophy. He considered his friend William Morris, to be "half a Positivist" and Walt Whitman a prophet of the new Positive Age that the humanity was about to enter.

If we are to take anything from Susan Lushington's statement regarding her father's restricted reading, it must surely endorse *Adam Bede* as the most Positivistic of all Eliot's works.

About the Contributor

David Taylor is an historian, writer and speaker. He is a Fellow of the Society of Antiquaries. He achieved his Masters, with a distinction, from Roehampton University, London. Later, after acquiring the important nineteenth-century Lushington family archive, Taylor successfully submitted his doctoral thesis *Vernon Lushington: Practising Positivism*. This was awarded the Blackham Fellowship in London and the Auguste Comte Prize in Paris. Subsequently he spent two years cataloguing the Lushington archive at the Surrey History Centre.

Taylor has appeared on television and has travelled widely both in the UK and the USA lecturing on various aspects of his doctoral thesis. His recently completed biography, *The Remarkable Lushington Family: Reformers, Pre-Raphaelites, and the Bloomsbury Group*, is to be published by Lexington Books

Chapter 18

George Eliot: Creating a Society's Back Story

Paul Davies

As you read any of George Eliot's novels you become aware that nearly all the characters have a depth and existence that goes far beyond the words on the page – they all have a back story – what has happened before the novel starts – of some complexity and we learn to understand them in quite extraordinary ways.

More than that, however, the reader becomes aware that the whole society in each of her novels has a back story – giving an even greater depth to the experience of reading the novels. And for me, this is one of the highly distinctive qualities of Eliot's novels.

Let's start with her characters and their back stories.

It's not that they are usually particularly likeable. Even my favourite character, Daniel Deronda, is – as is typical of quite a few of her male characters – quite a prig, remote, superior, aimless for much of the novel and pretty much a cold fish. Learning why the characters are like this and watching them start to grow into more rounded human beings is one of the fascinations of her novels – and we learn to appreciate her people warts and all as if they are real friends.

The women characters are flawed in a different way from the main male characters – especially if they are pretty – and, however attractive they might be, they all seem dangerous to me. They also have to fight hard to show their independence and capabilities.

I was almost immediately fascinated by her three dimensional characters – and equally fascinated to see how Eliot created them.

As I struggled with the question of how she implied so much detail about her characters, I became aware of one of her methods.

As you read George Eliot's novels, you may see that legal matters and legal issues are threaded through the novels – and you might wonder what this is all about.

I'm not referring to the litigation and criminal law that runs through the books, but the thread of legal connections embodied in land law which is most visible in *Felix Holt* and more subtly handled in *Daniel Deronda*.

(Mind you, there is enough of the other types of law as well, for example, in *The Mill on the* Floss, where Mr Tulliver unwisely insists on pursuing litigation to his own detriment, and there is a trial for murder in *Adam Bede*.)

Such legal complications can drive the action in many Victorian novels especially when it comes to the reading of wills, but when the legal paraphernalia is so complex, as it is in *Felix Holt*, and so innocuous as far as the plot is concerned, there's obviously something else going on.

There has been quite a focus on whether George Eliot got the land law right – and it has caused some unjustified academic controversy over the years, as we shall see.

I'm actually more concerned with what colour, depth, and insights her use of land law bring to the novel. In short – what was she doing.

Complicated Land Law

One of George Eliot's lesser read novels, *Felix Holt the Radical* was published in 1866. Most readers today will be hard pressed to see much that is radical about the character Felix Holt, but some of that incomprehension is caused by the remoteness of the issues in the book.

It is set in 1832, at the time of the Great Reform Act, and was written in the year before the Second Reform Act that was eventually passed in1867. Against the political fevers of that time a fairly conventional, apparently hopeless, love story plays out between a stubborn, proud and really self-opinionated Felix – there's no surprise there – and Esther, the step-daughter of the Reverend Rufus Lyon, a non-conformist minister.

The complex land law issues in *Felix Holt* are largely inexplicable today – even to those familiar with UK law – as an Act of Parliament in 1925 swept away most of the ideas behind life interests, entails and remainder men. They were not that explicable in 1866 as the Act for the Abolition of Fines and Recoveries of 1833 had removed many arcane practices.

In a nutshell, the way that Esther unwittingly becomes the heiress to the Transome fortune is complex and depends upon a tightly constructed legal framework. One of the Transome descendants sold his life interest[1] in the estate to a man called Durfey without getting his father's agreement to the sale (life interests and the original will could only be defeated if two generations agreed).

Under the terms of the original will, if the Transomes die out, then the life interest goes to a cousin of the original Transome, Henry Bycliffe, and afterwards his heirs.

In the novel Durfey has changed his name confusingly but typically to Transome, and the original Transomes, now fallen on hard times, have become Trounsems.

When the last Trounsem dies, the Bycliffes become the ultimate remainder men (or women), the Durfey-Transome ownership of the fortune is forfeit, and as Esther is the latest representative of the Bycliffe family, she inherits the estate.

All very complex and confusing. And disputed at the time whether it was proper law. This was initially anonymously in the *Edinburgh Review* written by G S Venables, a lawyer. His grounds were partly based on the Statute of Limitations which imposed a twenty year legal time limit and a good deal more than twenty years had passed.

Nevertheless, as you might imagine, George Eliot had researched this thoroughly and her lawyer friend, Frederick Harrison, had substantiated the legal apparatus. And a letter in the *Pall Mall Gazette*, under the soubriquet A Mouldy Conveyancer, rejected Venables' arguments but the dispute has rumbled on

---

[1] A life interest was just that – a person, usually a man, inherited a property and had the use of it for life, and on death that interest wasn't for that individual to assign but it went to the personage already designated in the original will to have a life interest.

and occasionally it's still used to undermine George Eliot's competence.

Unsurprisingly George Eliot, and her friend, Harrison, were right and in an 1896 standard legal work, *The Land Laws*, by Sir Frederick Pollock, a barrister expert on conveyancing, there is a definitive judgment which says that George Eliot was absolutely right, giving apparently irrefutable justifications.[2]

So far quite an academic storm in a teacup – a teacup reduced to a thimble by the fact that at the very moment Esther becomes the heiress she gives it all up. None of the legal superstructure seems to make any difference and could be a complete waste of time

So what on earth was going on in the author's mind and in the novel?

Especially as George Eliot had written to Harrison at the start of his research:

> The moral necessities of the situation might
> be met by the fact of injustice and foul play
> towards B [in this case Esther]; but I should
> prefer the legal claim if possible.[3]

Let's pause to have a look at *Daniel Deronda* where land law is lurking in the text in two significant places rather than being a driver of the plot.

For her last novel, George Eliot again consulted her friend Frederick Harrison about land law, and some critics, reading her letters have rather confused matters thinking her first to him question is focused on Daniel Deronda, himself, when in fact she's asking about

---

[2] Sir Frederick Pollock, *The Land Laws*, MacMillan, London, 1896

[3] George Eliot Letters, V4, 9th January 1866 GE to FH

Grandcourt's illegitimate son, Henleigh. It's actually a simple question about what happens to Grandcourt's estate if Henleigh were to become legitimate. No controversy there.

There's slightly more complexity in the other question which is about whether Sir Hugo Mallinger can buy out Grandcourt's right-in-tail to the house Mallinger has a life interest in, as Mallinger only has daughters and the will requires him to have a male heir to maintain his heirs' life interest in the house.

The answer is that if he wants to buy Grandcourt out, and Grandcourt is willing to sell, he can.

It's that two generation agreement thing again.

There's obviously not much here to frighten the horses or detain the average reader, especially as it is more subtle and less obvious in *Daniel Deronda* than in *Felix Holt*, although unlike the earlier novel it does have a real function in the plot – so what is going on?

We can see several things that it is *not* almost immediately.

Often when the law is introduced into a novel as a driver, there is some sort of conflict between justice and the law. Doesn't occur here, as far as I know, though you might feel that Sir Hugo's daughters have a pretty rough deal just because they are women.

We've also seen that, particularly in *Felix Holt*, the legal complications have little or no impact on the plot or story.

It seemed to me when I was first contemplating all of this, that whatever the meaning of land law was in the novels, it was closely related to something deep inside Eliot's consciousness.

One explanation is that George Eliot always was a stickler for accuracy and researched her issues tirelessly (as those of us who have read *Romola* set in the Florence of Savonarola perhaps know only too well).

One clue as to what is going on is in that letter to Frederick Harrison in 1875, when she is writing *Daniel Deronda*:

> But I hope that through your kindness I may be able to understand what were the family affairs of my personages – for such understanding is necessary to my comfort, if not to the true relation of that part of their history which I undertake to write.

The use of the word *comfort* is really important, and I see it as the vital link in understanding both what she's doing and how she does it, as is her debt to Sir Walter Scott who is actually quite a Tulliver figure with the ruinous litigation that forced him to write novels.

George Henry Lewes, her partner, wrote to Alexander MacMillan in 1878:

> . . Scott is to her an almost sacred name . .[4]

Scott, himself a lawyer, had great fun with the law and lawyers and in *Waverley* has a plot device centered on entail and life interests and male primogeniture, in the character of Bradwardine, which has strong echoes in *Daniel Deronda*. In his book on Scott[5] by one of my favourite contemporary reviewers of George Eliot's novels, Richard Holt Hutton writes:

> . . . to say nothing of his interest in [the law] as an antiquarian and historian who loved to re-people the earth, not merely with the

---

[4] George Eliot Letters, V7, 26th August 1878 GHL to AM
[5] R H Hutton, *Sir Walter Scott*, Macmillan, London 1907, p26

picturesque groups of the soldiers and courts of the past, but with the actors in all the various quaint and homely transactions and puzzlements which the feudal ages had brought forth.

Pollock gives a further insight into this:

> From the latter part of [the thirteenth] century onwards the system underwent a series of grave modifications. Grave as these were, however, the main lines of feudal theory were always ostensibly preserved.[6]

Interesting word *feudal*.

Twenty years or so before she wrote her last novel, George Eliot had reviewed two books by Wilhelm Heinrich von Riehl for the *Westminster Review*.

There was this telling paragraph:

> It is the same with historical traditions. The peasant has them fresh in his memory, so far as they relate to himself. In districts where the peasantry are unadulterated, you discern the remnants of the feudal relations in innumerable customs and phrases . .[7]

It's not that George Eliot wanted a return to feudalism – there is no hint of that – but she did want stability in a world that was becoming increasingly unstable.

There's something of a clue in this view of Grandcourt in *Daniel Deronda*:

---

[6] Sir Frederick Pollock, *The Land Laws*, MacMillan, London, 1896 p53

[7] GE, "The Natural History of German Life" *Westminster Review*, July 1856, volume LXVI pp51-59

> Grandcourt's importance as a subject of this
> realm was of the grandly passive kind which
> consists in the inheritance of land.[8]

At no point could you make an argument for George
Eliot admiring Grandcourt. And this quotation has a
great deal of irony flowing through it because of that,
but there is a sense of continuity and solidity about the
not only unchanging but almost immutable status of
land owning.

If you think about the time when George Eliot was
writing *Felix Holt*, with the uncertainty in her mind
over the Secord Reform Act, and consider how *Daniel
Deronda*, set it appears some twenty years before her
time of writing, and obviously much more in people's
consciousness and think about the changes in wealth
creation, transport and political activity, it isn't
surprising to me that at the very least she wanted to find
something in society that glued it together and would
stop everything falling apart.

George Eliot was too attached to meliorism, as we
can see particularly well in *Middlemarch*, to be a
reactionary just wanting to stop history and take away
its effects on society. UK land law – that remnant of the
old, unseen bonds between people, harking back to the
feudal system (which Eliot agreed was in its time a
progressive element for society) – provided a strong
sense of the security and strength of society.

The interplay in *Daniel Deronda*, in particular,
between the need for change and the longing for
stability – seen best in how she treats the role of women,

---

[8] *Daniel Deronda*, Cabinet Edition *The Works of George Eliot*,
21 Volumes, Blackwood and Sons, Edinburgh and London 1878-
1884, V3, Chapter 48, p59

especially in Gwendolen's path through life – is fascinating.

I can't leave this without a quotation from *Daniel Deronda* that I've enjoyed over the years, (especially now with a son who is a lawyer):

"How very nice!" said Gwendolen, with a concealed scepticism as to niceness in general, which made the word quite applicable to lawyers[9]

So I think there are two reasons underpinning Eliot's use of land law, and they are not related to developing or driving her plots as you might expect.

The first is that it gives her a depth to her characters, linking them to the past and tying together the various members of society with unseen but no less tangible strands. It is a back story for each individual character and a back story for the whole society which she is depicting. In *Felix Holt* especially the various members of society across a range of classes are actually tied together by land law relationships, so rich and poor, aristocrat and peasant have a common interest in a world of massive social mobility.

Secondly, underneath the vast changes in society that were quite disturbing to Eliot but which she did not resist, there was a level of continuity and sameness which was re-assuring. Land law was changing and changes had been made in Eliot's lifetime – but the strength of relationships that land law imposed on her characters, especially in *Daniel Deronda*, meant that

---

[9] *Daniel Deronda*, Cabinet Edition *The Works of George Eliot*, 21 Volumes, Blackwood and Sons, Edinburgh and London 1878-1884, V3, Chapter 44, p12

change was not going to be revolutionary, overthrowing everything, but a gradual process.

This can best be seen in an interesting piece of Eliot's writing. Her publisher, John Blackwood, at the time of the Second Reform Act, in 1867 just after the publication of *Felix Holt*, asked her if she might write a short address to working men. The outcome was *Address to Working Men*, ostensibly by her character, Felix Holt. In it Felix writes:

> He might as well say that there is no better rule needful for men that each should tug and rive for what will please him, without caring how that tugging will act on the fine widespread network of society in which he is fast meshed.[10]

And, finally, to reinforce an idea of land law being *incarnate history*, there is this:

> Thus in 1850 when History was first given status as a subject suitable for academic study at Oxford, it was as part of a combined school of law and history.[11]

I hope exploring how she uses land law is a spur to seeing how George Eliot created her worlds while also helping her readers appreciate her brilliance and control of her imagined societies and perhaps tease out other ways she creates a social back story.

---

[10] George Eliot *Address to Working Men, by Felix Holt, Blackwood's Magazine*, January 1868,ciii pp1-11 (reprinted T. Pinney (editor), *Essays of George Eliot*, pp416-30 – p49. Columbia University Press and Routledge and Kegan Paul 1963)

[11] Arthur Marwick *The Nature of History*, MacMillan, London 1970, p46.

By adding to our perception of the layers of meaning and the connections with ideas in her novels I hope it enhances the experience of reading them, and shows how lightly, effectively and, perhaps, deceptively, George Eliot uses her profound knowledge and creates a solidity in her depiction of society that is usually subliminal but also highly effective.

About the Contributor

Paul Davies is the Editor of this book and his details can be seen at the beginning. This article is based on a chapter from his doctoral dissertation: *George Eliot: Interpretations of a Society*.

Chapter 19

George Eliot and German Literature

John Rignall

Although I first read *Middlemarch* (1871–2) immediately after finishing my undergraduate studies in Modern Languages, I did not really get to grips with George Eliot's masterpiece until I taught it in a university course on the European Novel a few years later. In that context it took its proper place alongside Flaubert's *Madame Bovary* (1857) and Tolstoy's *Anna Karenina* (1873–7) as one of the great works of European realism in the nineteenth century.

George Eliot herself invites us to read her novel as belonging to the literature of Europe by heading each chapter with an epigraph drawn from writers such as Chaucer and Dante, Shakespeare and Cervantes, Goethe and Victor Hugo.

With my knowledge of German literature I found the Goethe epigraph particularly intriguing. It heads Chapter 81 at the moral climax of Dorothea's life, when, despite her anguish at suspecting Ladislaw is involved in an illicit relationship with Rosamond Lydgate, she goes to visit Rosamond to see what she can do to help, and is rewarded by being told by Rosamond that, she, Dorothea, is the only woman Ladislaw loves.

The quotation from Goethe consists of a few lines from the beginning of his *Faust, Part II* (1832) when Faust, awakening from a healing sleep, resolves from now on to strive continually towards the highest form of existence. This epigraph invites us to see a connection between the personal moral struggle of a young woman of the English provincial upper middle class and Faust's ruthless quest for knowledge and experience which embodies the dynamic, thrusting individualism of European modernity.

It is worth noting that Dorothea has one ambition that is directly reminiscent of Faust's, 'to take a great deal of land, and drain it, and make a little colony' (*Middlemarch*, Ch. 55); but in her case it is simply philanthropic and has none of Faust's corrupting drive for power and lust for boundless experience. Moreover, whereas Faust's resolution to strive upwards comes after a sleep that grants him convenient oblivion to his guilty part in the death of Gretchen, whom he has seduced and got with child, Dorothea's follows an anguished night of wakefulness that is the mark of the developed moral consciousness in George Eliot's world, where characters are typically not permitted to bury the past and escape the consequences of their actions.

Thus this allusion to Goethe in *Middlemarch* shows both her familiarity with one of the great works of German literature and at the same time her readiness to adapt Goethe's example for her own purposes, giving a moral inflection to Faustian striving and re-imagining it as a woman's ideal.

It is significant that this reference to German literature is to a poetic drama rather than to a novel, since in George Eliot's lifetime there was no tradition of German novel-writing to match those of Britain, France, or Russia. As George Eliot's partner, the versatile writer G. H. Lewes, put it in an 1858 article on 'Realism in Art: Recent German Fiction', 'the novels of Germany are singularly inferior to those of France and England' and 'are, for the most part, dreary inflictions' because they have so little realism (*Westminster Review*, Vol. 70, p. 491).

George Eliot assisted Lewes with his article by reading and discussing the German works with him and she no doubt agreed with his judgment. One writer who escapes Lewes's dismissive criticism is the Swiss-German Gottfried Keller and his collection of stories, *The People of Seldwyla* (1856). Keller was an exact contemporary of George Eliot and was living in Berlin in 1854–5 when she and Lewes were there on their first visit to Germany. Although they had at least one acquaintance in common, they never met, but one of Keller's stories which Lewes singles out for special attention, 'A Village Romeo and Juliet', was read by George Eliot in 1858 and has some interesting thematic affinities with the novel she was to begin writing in the following year, *The Mill on the Floss* (1860). Keller's young couple are the offspring of neighbouring peasants who fall out with each other, and the hopelessness of their predicament causes the young lovers finally to choose to die together by slipping into the river after a night of love on a hay-barge.

This fable-like story is very different from George Eliot's richly circumstantial and expansive novel, but there are enough elements in common – a family feud, destructive litigation, death by drowning, and the association of the river with the current of desire – to suggest that George Eliot's reading of it may have played some part in the genesis of *The Mill on the Floss*.

As for German novels, the ones that were important for her were Goethe's. In *The Mill on the Floss* the title of the chapter in which Maggie and Stephen Guest begin to be attracted to each other, 'Illustrating the Laws of Attraction' (Bk 6, Ch. 6), is a direct reference to the subject matter and the title of Goethe's novel of adulterous love, *Elective Affinities* (1809), which alludes to the chemical laws according to which substances are drawn to each other.

There is also an echo of Goethe in another climactic moment in *Middlemarch* when Dorothea and Will Ladislaw are finally brought together by a convenient thunderstorm and a flash of lightning that causes them to clasp hands 'like two children, looking out on the storm' (Ch. 83). Readers of Goethe will be reminded of his novel of ill-fated romantic love, *The Sorrows of Young Werther* (1774), and the first meeting of Werther and Lotte, the object of the hero's hopeless infatuation, when the two figures both respond to a thunderstorm in the same way and are brought together by a spontaneous allusion to a German poet. In both scenes there is a self-conscious use of the romantic cliché of the storm in the handling of the characters and the development of their relationship.

The Goethe novel that was most important for George Eliot is *Wilhelm Meister's Apprenticeship* (1795–6), the archetype of the *Bildungsroman*, or novel of formation, that traces a young character's early steps into the adult world. In July 1855 she wrote a short article on the novel, 'The Morality of Wilhelm Meister' , in the *Leader* (*Essays of George Eliot*, pp. 143–7) to help promote Lewes's biography of Goethe which was about to be published.

In defending the novel against the widely held view in Britain that it was an immoral book, she praised Goethe's large tolerance as the mark of his moral superiority, and when she describes how he presents us with 'living, generous humanity—mixed and erring, and self-deluding, but saved from utter corruption' by some redeeming feature (*Essays*, p. 146), she is describing in advance what she is also going to achieve in her own fiction, which she began to write in the following year.

Goethe's benignly ironic, non-judgmental treatment of his characters and his ability to inspire sympathy for a wide range of human character and behaviour, remained a lasting inspiration for her.

A more specific debt to *Wilhelm Meisters's Apprenticeship* appears in her last novel, *Daniel Deronda* (1876), where Daniel's aspirations allude directly to Goethe's model: 'He longed now to have the sort of apprenticeship to life which would not shape him too definitely, and rob him of that choice that might come from a free growth' (Ch. 16). And like Wilhelm, he is indeed granted the freedom to grow and has mentors to guide him, and in contrast to Gwendolen and the hardship of her woman's lot, he is, like Goethe's hero, a peculiarly privileged being.

The only other German writer George Eliot wrote about in critical articles was the poet Heinrich Heine. In 1855 and 1856 she wrote four pieces in different journals, the most substantial and important being 'German Wit: Heinrich Heine' published in the *Westminster Review* in January 1856, which was largely responsible for introducing Heine to the English-speaking world.

Heine was Jewish and George Eliot found him in some respects unlike other German writers, defining the difference by likening him in part to a French writer: his prose is 'as light and subtle and needle-pointed as Voltaire's French' while his poetical style is 'as crystalline, as graceful, and as musical as that of Goethe's best lyrics (*Leader*, Vol. 6, p. 843).

She particularly admired Heine's lyric poetry but, while acknowledging the power of his satirical wit, she seemed less comfortable with his self-conscious irony and was more inclined to celebrate his tender lyrics than to appreciate the complex divided self that he reveals in his poetry.

She noted his commitment to freedom and democracy but saw that his wit prevented him from ever being a thorough-going partisan of any cause, and she drew attention to his refusal to align himself with any party, whether republican or patriotic, Christian or Jew. However, when in her last novel, *Daniel Deronda*, she came to deal with Jews and Judaism, it was precisely his Jewishness that made his work an important resource and she drew particularly on the 'Hebrew Melodies' in his collection *Romanzero* (1851).

It was probably Heine's poem on Jehuda ben Halevy that led her to that medieval Jewish poet who inspires the visionary Mordecai's Hebrew verses in the novel (Ch. 38); and when the Jewish musician Klesmer declares his love for Catherine Arrowpoint, he softly plays the melody of his own setting of Heine's poem 'I have loved you and love you still' (Ch. 22). Three of the chapter epigraphs are drawn from Heine (Chs 34, 62, 63), two of them on Jewish themes.

The only other German literary figures referred to or cited in *Daniel Deronda* are Goethe and the poet and playwright Friedrich Schiller.

Schiller was an early enthusiasm of George Eliot's when she first learnt German in the early 1840s. She read all of his plays and much of his poetry and found his idealism and portrayals of heroic humanity inspiring. It has been suggested that *The Mill on the Floss* owes something to Schiller in Maggie's heroic insistence on being true to herself, while in *Daniel Deronda* Mirah claims that she learned evil and good from reading Shakespeare and Schiller.

Another eighteenth-century German dramatist, Gotthold Ephraim Lessing, may also have had some influence on the subject-matter of *Daniel Deronda* since his play about a Jew, *Nathan the Wise* (1779), with its appeal for religious tolerance, was much admired by George Eliot who found that its 'noble words' brought tears to her eyes when she first saw it in Berlin many years earlier (*Journals of George Eliot*, p. 249). She also admired Lessing's work as a critic, finding his writing most un-German in its clarity and liveliness in *Laokoon* (1766) where he draws a masterly distinction between poetry and the plastic arts which informs the argument about poetry and painting in *Middlemarch* (Ch. 19), when Ladislaw proclaims to the painter Naumann that language is a finer medium than painting.

German literature was for George Eliot one of the three greatest literatures of the world, along with English and French, and she read widely in it throughout her career. Goethe was the most important German writer for her, and she found in his work a tolerant wisdom, breadth and profundity that were an enduring source of inspiration.

In the last months of her life she was re-reading the first part of *Faust* with her husband John Cross, who reported in his biography of the novelist that nothing in literature moved her more deeply than the tragic figure of Gretchen, who touched her more than anything in Shakespeare. Germany's greatest writer was thus of central importance to George Eliot, but her own work, although well-known in Germany, does not seem to have left its mark on any major German writers, in contrast to France, where Marcel Proust, André Gide, and Simone de Beauvoir were great admirers.

About the Contributor

John Rignall, John Rignall is Reader Emeritus in English and Comparative Literary Studies at the University of Warwick. His publications include *Realist Fiction and the Strolling Spectator* (1992), *George Eliot, European Novelist* (2011), and, as editor, *George Eliot and Europe* (1997), the Everyman Paperback edition of *Daniel Deronda* (1999), *The Oxford Reader's Companion to George Eliot* (2000) and, with H. Gustav Klaus, *Ecology and the Literature of the British Left* (2012). He is also co-editor of the *George Eliot Review*..

Chapter 20

Here Be Dragons:
George Eliot's Self-Made Heroes

Shoshana Milgram Knapp

When I think of my favourite moments in George Eliot, I picture characters standing on a crucial threshold. Their eyes are open wide, their minds engaged, their spirits solemn. They welcome the difficulty ahead; they embrace the danger. They resemble the long-ago explorers attracted by map notations indicating the presence of perils: *Here be dragons.*

In the dawn of a decision, they are ready and eager. I cannot wait to see what they will do next, and I cannot look away.

The choices that confront George Eliot's characters are the fundamental alternatives that we all face: to live bravely or to surrender, to reach for the noblest possible to us or to settle for less. Her fiction aims a dramatic spotlight at the times when one can shape an entire life course by seeing clearly and acting bravely. Her insight is contrary to the conventional view that morality requires self-denial. The heroic life—and it is a life available to all thinking beings—is one of self-affirmation. It requires respect for the demands of one's best self; it asks one to hear and heed the highest voice within.

George Eliot offers the reader the intimate privilege of watching her men and women weigh their options and embark upon a heroic life. It is an adventure each person must choose independently. And yet, in her fiction as in our own experience, another person can provide counsel, support, and inspiration. Heroism is not an easy life, and is all the better for not being easy.

The effort itself is part of the reward.

Meet Tertius Lydgate, for example: twenty-seven years young. He falls in love at first sight not with a woman, but with medicine. One day, by chance, he reads in an encyclopaedia a passage about the valves of the heart. Those valves, metaphorically, open the way to a whole new world:

He knew that valves were folding doors, and through this crevice came a sudden light startling him with his first vivid notion of finely adjusted mechanism in the human frame. . . But the moment of vocation had come, and before he got down from his chair, the world was made new to him by a presentiment of endless processes filling the vast spaces planked out of his sight by that wordy ignorance which he had supposed to be knowledge. From that hour Lydgate felt the growth of an intellectual passion.

(*Middlemarch*, Chapter 15)

Lydgate recognizes how much there is to learn about the human body.

Challenge accepted, on behalf of Lydgate's best self.

He aspires to be a discoverer, an explorer of "vast spaces". On the map of his personal ambition, he targets the areas of most intense risk. In accordance with the "sudden light startling him," he intends to illuminate the most significant issues of human life and human health.

Here be dragons!

He is not afraid of hard questions; he invites them. He is not afraid of questioning the status quo; he cheerfully anticipates being the voice of reform. He even has a practical plan for navigating between the eternal and the everyday. By setting up practice in a provincial town, he "seeks to do good small work for Middlemarch, and great work for the world."

Does he succeed or fail? The narrator warns us, in general terms, that much can intervene between the pursuit of a worthy goal and its achievement.

A good number who once meant to shape their own deeds and alter the world a little. The story of their coming to be shapen after the average and fit to be packed after the gross, is hardly ever told even in their consciousness, for perhaps their ardour in generous unpaid toil cooled as imperceptibly as the ardour of other youthful loves, till one day their earlier self walked like a ghost in its old home and made the new furniture ghastly.

(*Middlemarch* Chapter 15)

Some people who intended to reform the world find that, instead, they have been worn down into conformity; their new lives are a dreary setting for their "earlier self."

But if this is the sad fate of a "good number," it is not necessarily the tragedy in store for our Lydgate. What threats might he encounter, in his home or community or the solitude of his own mind? What might make him vulnerable? How might he protect his best self? How can he remain true to the "intellectual passion" that had changed his life's course? How can he perform the unrelenting labour required to discover and apply the relevant facts about human physiology?

George Eliot asks the questions, and we observe the answers.

Along the way, when his courage falters and he begins to doubt himself, he encounters a priceless gift: the understanding of a fellow creature who knows what he meant to be:

The presence of a noble nature, generous in its wishes, ardent in its charity, changes the lights for us: we begin to see things again in their larger, quieter masses, and to believe that we too can be seen and judged in the wholeness of our character. This influence was beginning to act on Lydgate, who had for many days been seeing all life as one who is dragged and struggling amid the throng. He sat down again, and felt that he was recovering his old self in the consciousness that he was with one who believed in it.

(*Middlemarch*, Chapter 76)

In seeing himself judged "in the wholeness of his character," he recovers "his old self," sees "again" the truth about himself and his world, and can contemplate the prospect of going forward in the footsteps of his "intellectual passion." Whatever his future, he remembers the heroic vocation that he embraced at twenty-seven, and that he never intended to abandon.

What next? Wait and see.

Another of George Eliot's explorers is Esther Lyon, a young woman of marriageable age and marriageable temperament. In the concluding chapters of *Felix Holt, the Radical*, the intricacies of the plot (involving decades-old secrets of paternity and identity, along with a tangled thread of inheritance) appear to place Esther in the position of choosing between two suitors of contrasting backgrounds, convictions, and views of her.

This, however, is not in fact the essence of her choice. Esther Lyon, on the threshold of a crucial decision, is choosing not between two partners, but between two lives, two futures, two views of herself. Esther's decision centrally concerns the aspiration of her best self toward a heroic life, the highest (and hardest) life for her.

Throughout the novel, Felix Holt has asked Esther to take life and herself seriously, rather than "giving [her] soul up to trifles" (Chapter 10, 210). She wonders if she can do this:

Did he [Felix] want her to be heroic? That seemed impossible without some great occasion. Her life was a heap of fragments, and so were her thoughts: some great energy was needed to bind them together"

(Chapter 16, 264).

Esther, admittedly, thinks of Felix's relation to her as potentially romantic, and therefore as involving her sharing both his life and his principles. If she did so, " . . her life would be exalted into something quite new—into a sort of difficult blessedness, such as one may imagine in beings who are conscious of painfully growing into possession of higher powers. (Chapter 22). That "difficult blessedness" represents her own personal sign of a challenge and a temptation.

Here be dragons.

When Esther comments that Felix appears to care little for himself, he explains just how wrong she is:

"You are thoroughly mistaken," said Felix. "It is just because I'm a very ambitious fellow, with very hungry passions, wanting a great deal to satisfy me, that I have chosen to give up what people call worldly good."

(Chapter 27)

Although he asks if she could "imagine [herself] choosing hardship as the better lot," he does not invite her to share his deeply personal ambitions, his "hungry passions."

What does he urge her to do? To live her *own* noble life. To live a heroic life entails guarding her best self from the risk of sliding into triviality. Felix tells Esther that he wants her to have a "vision," an inner projection of what it would mean to betray her heroic possibilities:

"I do believe in you; but I want you to have such a vision of the future that you may never lose your best self. Some charm or other may be flung about you— some of your attar-of-rose fascinations—and nothing but a good strong terrible vision will save you."

(Chapter 27)

The events of the plot, as if on cue, provide some "charm or other," in the form of Harold Transome, who believes it is a man's function to protect a woman from any trouble, who embodies "masculine ease" and who offers her no more than "a life of middling delights, overhung with the languorous haziness of motiveless ease" (Chapter 44).

Her choice, indeed, appears to be the choice between Felix and Harold, but it is actually a choice between the highest life and something else, something less.

There was something which she now felt profoundly to be the best thing that life could give her. But—if it was to be had at all—it was not to be had without paying a heavy price for it, such as we must pay for all that is greatly good.

A supreme love, a motive that gives a sublime rhythm to a woman's life, and exalts habit into partnership with the soul's highest needs, is not to be had where and how she wills: to know that high initiation, she must often tread where it is hard to tread, and feel the chill air, and watch through darkness. It is not true that love makes all things easy: it makes us choose what is difficult.

(Chapter 49)

True, "she might find herself on the stony road alone." Whether or not she marries Felix, the highest life is what it is, and so is the lesser life.

And on the other side there was a lot where everything seemed easy—but for the fatal absence of those feelings which, now she had once known them, it seemed nothing less than a fall and degradation to do without.

The heroic life is exalted and hard; the alternative is degraded and easy. Felix has inspired her to see clearly what she wants, who she can be, and what the choice constitutes, but the choice pertains to Esther's own nature. What can she do? What will she do? What should she do?

This chapter's epigraph places a thumb on the scale and states unambiguously that the choice of the "noblest" is the certain good and the sole good:

> Nay, falter not—'tis an assured good
> To seek the noblest—'tis your only good
> Now you have seen it; for that higher vision
> Poisons all meaner choice forevermore.

Who, though, is the speaker?

The poetic language is not typical of the plain-spoken Felix. Perhaps we are hearing the voice of the novel's wise narrator, or the wise novelist. Perhaps this is the voice of an ideal friend, seeing Esther in the fullness of her character, and calling on her to sustain her "higher vision" in order to live bravely the higher life.

This epigraph puts in words what Esther has understood for herself and by herself: that her alternative is indeed absolute, that the best, once seen, makes anything less unthinkable.

George Eliot's poetry expresses the inspiration of the call to heroism. The same exhortation is addressed to us as human beings and as readers. The heroic life is not easy, but it is worth it.

And George Eliot's fiction is not easy, either. It asks much of us. It asks us to rise to the occasion. And if we "choose what is difficult," we too can achieve "the best thing life can give."

When I think of her characters on the threshold, I remember not only her epigraph, but also a powerful expression of the same warning from a philosopher who, notoriously, disparaged George Eliot, but who, in his own voice, expresses the same wisdom: embracing one's best self entails fleeing the meanest, and reaching for the highest.

> Ah! I have known noble men who lost their highest hope. And then they disparaged all high hopes.
> Then lived they shamelessly in temporary pleasures, and beyond the day had hardly an aim.
> . . . Then broke the wings of their spirit; and now it creeps about, and defileth where it gnaweth.

Once they thought of becoming heroes; but sensualists are they now. A trouble and a terror is the hero to them.

But by my love and hope I conjure thee: cast not away the hero in thy soul! Maintain holy thy highest hope!—

(Friedrich Nietzsche, *Thus Spake Zarathustra*, First Part, Chapter VIII "The Tree on the Hill," translated by Thomas Common, originally published in 1911, New York: Dover, 1999, 26-27)

About the contributor

Shoshana Milgram Knapp teaches literature and film at Virginia Tech. Her publications on George Eliot include articles in *Nineteenth-Century Fiction*, *Victorian Newsletter*, and *Slavic and East European Journal*. She has also published articles on, among others, Hugo, Napoleon, George Sand, Dostoevsky, Chekhov, Alexandra Kollontai, Victoria Cross, E. L. Voynich, Steinbeck, Richard Wright, Max Eastman, Ursula K. Le Guin, and Ayn Rand (about whom she is completing a book-length study).

Chapter 21

George Eliot's Passionate Energy in Describing the Universe

Eri Satoh

Why have George Eliot's works continued to attract me for more than ten years? That's a difficult question for me to answer but well worth trying to.

I sometimes recall my first encounter with *Middlemarch* in the fourth year of undergraduate college. I cannot clearly remember why I decided to tackle this *great masterpiece*. However, some mysterious motivation urged me to read it. As I had expected, it was hard to get through all the volumes and understand the content with my limited knowledge, but I was fascinated by Dorothea Brooke's personality and the vital descriptions of her experience, such as her marriage with Edward Casaubon and her romance and remarriage with Will Ladislaw.

At the same time, I was really encouraged by the famous passage in 'Finale' in which Eliot compares the life of Dorothea with that of St. Theresa:

> But the effect of [Dorothea's] being on those around her was incalculably diffusive: for the growing good of the world is partly dependent on unhistoric acts; and that things are not so ill with you and me as they might have been, is half owing to the number who

lived faithfully a hidden life, and rest in unvisited tombs.
(Middlemarch, Finale)

I did not know much about Eliot's religious background when I read *Middlemarch*, but I was greatly encouraged by her philosophy. At that time, I was thinking about my career after graduation. I had already decided to enter graduate school, but I was asking myself how I could contribute to society by continuing my research.

This reading experience opened up my way to life as a researcher of English Literature which, I believe became a vocation for me. Since then, I have repeatedly read *Middlemarch* and continued a dialogue with Eliot and her works. Eliot has always helped me to expand my thirst for knowledge and enrich my life.

A Remarkable Ability to Describe Society and Human Nature

What is particularly remarkable is the faculty of Eliot's visions – both mental and physical. Her observation is both macroscopic and microscopic. With a fabulous ability to perceive the world, her ways of seeing are similar to those of a scientist, geographer, painter, musician, sociologist, and anthropologist. Sometimes she mentions important historical events and weaves the vast human network in society through her language. In her later novels, such as *Middlemarch* and *Daniel Deronda,* a large number of characters appear and all of them are connected with each other in some ways. At other times, on a microscopic level, she penetrates the labyrinth of complex and mysterious human psychology, for example, Mr Casaubon's inner struggle as an isolated scholar.

Her ability to anatomize human nature is remarkable. In my opinion, no other authors fully understand the inconsistency of human nature like Eliot:

> (Every nerve and muscle in Rosamond was adjusted to the consciousness that she was being looked at. She was by nature an actress of parts that entered into her *physique*: she even acted her own character, and so well, that she did not know it to be precisely her own.)
>
> (Middlemarch, Ch 12)

In this passage, Eliot depicts not only Rosamond's unstable personality but also the essence of human nature because true self is extremely difficult to define.

As another example, Mr Farebrother says:

> 'character is not cut in marble – it is not something solid and unalterable. It is something living and changing, and may become diseased as our bodies do.'
>
> (Middlemarch, Ch 72)

In *Daniel Deronda*, the narrator says:

> Attempts at description are stupid: who can all at once describe a human being? even when he is presented to us we only begin that knowledge of his appearance which must be completed by innumerable impressions under differing circumstances.
>
> (*Daniel Deronda*, Book II, Ch 2)

In terms of human nature, Eliot's creation of Gwendolen Harleth in this novel is complex. Even though Gwendolen is from the same lineage as Hetty Sorrel in *Adam Bede* and Rosamond in *Middlemarch* with her extreme confidence in her beauty and vanity, she is also overly sensitive and has a conscience, which reinforces Eliot's untiring efforts to pursue the nature of human beings. Moreover, like Mr Casaubon's case, through Eliot's magical description, we are convinced to sympathize with a character, who did not seem attractive at first. She never classifies her characters by several stereotypes. (Grandcourt may be an exception, but even his creation can be seen as Eliot's one experiment).

Eliot's portrayal of characters does not depend on the simple dualistic value of gender seen in the Victorian period. Interestingly enough, Silas Marner engages in child-rearing, which was mainly conducted by women then. She created somewhat *feminine* heroes like Will Ladislaw and Daniel Deronda in her later two novels. In these two characters, Eliot seeks the equal male-female relationship in which both sexes can understand each other like friends.

Eliot also explores the preciousness and difficulty of sympathizing with each other in some forms of relationships, such as romantic relationships, marital relationships, and friendships between men and women. In *Middlemarch*, she describes the friendship between Dorothea and Lydgate, which seems to transcend the boundary of gender. In *Daniel Deronda*, the relationship between Deronda and Gwendolen is more problematic than in *Middlemarch*, as Eliot suggests their sexual attraction towards each other. Thus, in the later work, Eliot attempts to depict their relationship at a more unconscious level.

Once we begin reading her novels, we can wander into the labyrinths of society and human psychology.

George Eliot's Feminism in the Context of Modern Japanese Society

The female protagonists Eliot created are particularly attractive for me. One of my interests which helped me to decide on a theme for my doctoral thesis is so-called *dark women*, such as Caterina Sarti in *Mr Gilfil's Love Story*, Janet Dempster in *Janet's Repentance*, and Maggie Tulliver in *The Mill on the Floss*, for whom Simone de Beauvoir also expresses particular admiration.

They have not only dark eyes and dark hair but also passionate dispositions. As is often said, Eliot is harsh with female characters who are vain and conscious of their own beauty, such as Hetty and Rosamond. However, they are not simply foils of the female protagonists. (I can sympathize with George Eliot's harshness on the women who are conscious of their beauty and use it as their strength to attract men; women should be judged by their competence, not by their appearance.) Eliot's skilfully crafted omniscient narrator makes readers look at these female characters from different angles.

The question of women that Eliot deals with in her works never becomes obsolete, and it can be applied even in a modern Japanese context. Eliot never actively participated in her contemporary feminist movement, which has caused many to regard Eliot as ambiguous about the social advancement of women.

In Japan, women have advanced in society more than before, but they suffer the conventional values which the society imposes on them. For example, womanly tenderness beyond the familial ties which Eliot explores when Romola tends the sick Florentines still seem to be expected for working women in Japan.

In addition, the mother-daughter relationship which is specifically explored in *The Mill on the Floss* and *Daniel Deronda* also reflects one of the serious social problems in Japanese society. Even though Maggie is beyond her mother's control in her childhood, she grows up to be a beautiful woman (though her beauty is peculiar) as her mother expected. Gwendolen has to pretend to be happy in married life before her mother and always cares about her mother living at ease. They both tried to remain faithful to their mothers, instead of revealing their hidden criticism.

Beyond the Boundary of Countries

Eliot's abundant travel experiences make the scale of the novels larger and richer as her career as a novelist matures. Eliot chooses various kinds of places as the settings of her novels, particularly from *Romola* onward. She is the vigorous female fieldworker, walking along the seaside, going up the mountains and hills, and wandering into the woods. (These experiences must have served to help describe the natural world with a bird's eye view). She also visits galleries and museums, enjoys opera music and drama.

Like Eliot herself, the mobility of heroines in her novels is really impressive. In *Romola*, we can walk with Romola in Renaissance Florence. (Her meticulous study of Italian history in this novel is also surprising). With Dorothea we can visit Rome in *Middlemarch* and wander into the Vatican museum to appreciate the ancient statues. We also can visit Geneva with Deronda and enjoy sailing on the Mediterranean Sea with Gwendolen in *Daniel Deronda*. Mirah Lapidoth in *Daniel Deronda* also travels through the European continent to escape from her father's domination.

Reading Eliot's novels stimulates me to visit and walk around these fascinating European cities.

Every time I reread her novels, I not only reconfirm her greatness but also discover new facets and enjoy them from different angles.

Eliot's genius is in her astute descriptions of the complex social world and the mysteries of human nature.

Her works continue to live and thrive even in the modern context. By reading her novels, we can be absorbed into Eliot's descriptions of the universe brimming with her vigorous mental and physical energy.

About the Contributor

Eri Satoh earned a Ph.D. in English Literature from Kobe College in 2017 and she is now a part-time lecturer of English in the Department of English at Kobe College, Japan.

Her research interests include British women's fiction of the 19th century, especially George Eliot. In his doctoral thesis, she examined the descriptions of the heroines' visual experiences in George Eliot's novels, using George Henry Lewes's epistemological and psychological arguments. One of her recent articles is entitled "Self-Restoration and Imagination in 'Janet's Repentance' : Georg Eliot's Response to George Henry Lewes's Arguments on Perception" printed in *The George Eliot Review of Japan* 2017).

Chapter 22

Middlemarch and the Pleasures of the Everyday

Ben Moore

Middlemarch is one of the great monuments of British – and European – realism, but it is also a novel about the mundane ordinariness of everyday life, and indeed about failure.

Thinking of Saint Theresa of Avila, the sixteenth-century Spanish mystic depicted in a famous statue by Bernini, Eliot writes in the Prelude to the novel that 'Many Theresas have been born who found for themselves no epic life wherein there was a constant unfolding of far-resonant action; perhaps only a life of mistakes'.[1]

These lines seem to carry an echo of Thomas Gray's 'Elegy Written in a Country Churchyard', written over a century earlier, in which Gray reflects on the 'homely joys, and destiny obscure' of the many ordinary people who lie in unremembered graves across the English countryside.[2]

This is, admittedly, a rather sombre start to a chapter that claims to be interested in the *pleasures* rather than the *miseries* of the everyday, but my point is that one of

---

[1] George Eliot, *Middlemarch* (Peterborough, Ontario: Broadview, 2004), p. 31.

[2] Thomas Gray, 'Elegy Written in a Country Churchyard' (1751)

Eliot's achievements is to show that mistakes, failures and obscurities need not always be melancholic. There is something deeply affirmative in *Middlemarch*'s celebration of the rises and falls of ordinary life, its insistence that we pay close attention to the small moments whose accumulation shapes our experience of the world.

Everyday things – an awkward phrase, a badly-stitched collar, the choice of which jewellery to wear (or not to wear) – *matter* in Eliot's world. And in this respect her world is our world. The texture of everyday life she describes is still identifiably the place where we rub up against other people, and where other people rub up against us. It is the place where, willingly or not, we come into contact with the great currents of politics, culture, science and history, perhaps feeling their ripples at a great distance, without being fully conscious of what they mean.

As Eliot shows, we are all to some extent in the position of the ploughman in *Landscape with the Fall of Icarus* by Breughel the Elder (the surviving painting is perhaps a copy of his lost original), who continues to stare at the field he is farming while Icarus drops into the sea behind him. The mythical is brought down to earth, so to speak.

Like Breughel, Eliot is as interested in the texture of the soil and the placement of the farmer's feet as the divine fall of Icarus. As W.H. Auden puts it in his poem 'Musée des Beaux Arts', 'everything turns away/ Quite leisurely from the disaster; the ploughman may/ Have heard the splash, the forsaken cry,/ But for him it was not an important failure'.[3] Like Breughel and Auden, Eliot asks that we shift our perspective and adjust our

---

[3] W.H. Auden, 'Musée des Beaux Arts' (1940).

hierarchy of values, so that by a trick of the eye we come to see the background as foreground.

When we do so, even the most legendary failure is revealed to be part of a larger picture, in which normal life takes centre stage. It is no coincidence that Flemish and Dutch art was a favourite of hers.

Eliot's narrators hold the threads of this ordinary, frayed life up to view, and in doing so act like one of her most homely, and most sentimentalised, characters: Mrs Barton, who appears in the early story *Amos Barton*. Mrs Barton's fingers, we are told, are 'never empty',[4] so that whenever she visits her husband's parishioners, 'out came her thimble and a piece of calico or muslin, which, before she left, had become a mysterious little garment with all sorts of hemmed ins and outs'.[5]

This sewing of clothes symbolises Mrs Barton's stitching together of both her family and the wider community around her. Indeed, as Eliot's tale progresses, the texture of this community is itself shown to be a kind of 'mysterious little garment', with all sorts of 'ins and outs'.

Yet Mrs Barton is doomed to failure and domestic tragedy; the heap of 'undarned stockings' she needs to fix is never-ending,[6] and she ends the story buried beneath a tombstone that seems to come straight out of Gray's poem, where the grass has quickly 'grown long upon the grave', seeming to cover up all evidence of her life.[7]

---

[4] George Eliot, 'Amos Barton', in *Scenes of Clerical Life* (Oxford: OUP, 2015), p. 18.
[5] 'Amos Barton', p. 18.
[6] 'Amos Barton', p. 19.
[7] 'Amos Barton', p. 69.

Mrs Barton lives on, however, through the traces she leaves behind, especially the love that remains in her daughter Patty's heart. The point is clunkily made in this slightly unsatisfactory story of the 1850s, but by the time of *Middlemarch* we find a far richer and more sophisticated elaboration of the same idea.

In her most celebrated novel, Eliot casts a subtle light on the gossamer-thin strands that bind people together, what Wordsworth had earlier described as the 'feelings [...] Of unremembered pleasure' that 'have no slight or trivial influence/ On that best portion of a good man's life'.[8]

Of course, Eliot deals in pain, sadness and disappointment as well as pleasure, but these feelings are often knitted together inextricably in her writing. Sadness is rarely just sadness in *Middlemarch*. Instead, we get the 'benevolent sadness' of Mr Brooke as he commiserates with Mr Farebrother,[9] the 'affectionate sadness' of Mary Garth when she speaks to Fred after the reading of Mr Featherstone's will,[10] the 'dreary sadness' of Rosamond as she appeals to Will,[11] and most tellingly of all, Dorothea's belief that if only she were less ignorant about Rome, 'its sadness would have been winged with hope'.[12]

These sensations may be fleeting, but Eliot tries to catch them as they pass, even as they dissolve in her hands. This is maybe why Viriginia Woolf, one of the great modernist writers of the fleeting moment and the

---

[8] William Wordsworth, 'Lines Composed a Few Miles above Tintern Abbey, On Revisiting the Banks of the Wye during a Tour. July 13, 1798'.

[9] *Middlemarch*, p. 566.

[10] *Middlemarch*, p. 286.

[11] *Middlemarch*, p. 600.

[12] *Middlemarch*, p. 196.

half-felt impression, was so interested in Eliot, despite Woolf's desire to escape the stifling monumentality of the Victorian novel in novels like *To the Lighthouse*.

The small moments that shape our lives, and the lives of those around us, take myriad forms in *Middlemarch*. When Lydgate keeps his 'pencil suspended' in Chapter 18,[13] unsure up until the last moment whether he will vote for Mr Farebrother (whom he prefers) or Mr Tyke (who is preferred by Lydgate's powerful ally Bulstrode) to become chaplain of the new infirmary, the moment is both completely trivial and elevated into wider significance. His final decision is apparently prompted by the most arbitrary event, his annoyance at Mr Wrench commenting, 'I merely mean that you are expected to vote with Mr Bulstrode. Do you regard that meaning as offensive?'[14] Lydgate immediately writes down 'Tyke'.

Eliot's novel invites us to wonder how much this moment matters. Is it a momentous decision that will shape Lydgate's destiny, or an inevitable outcome of his previous choices? Is it the beginning of Lydgate's failure to live up to his ideals, or is that failure only really set in train by his later marriage to Rosamond? Eliot recognises the scale of the social and historical forces acting on Lydgate in this moment, but also the inconsequentiality of his choice, when she compares it to a man's selection of a new hat, which must be made 'from among such shapes as the resources of the age offer him'.[15]

Eliot is known for her serious intellectualism, but there is also a playfulness at work here. Although we

---

[13] *Middlemarch*, p. 172.
[14] *Middlemarch*, p. 172.
[15] *Middlemarch*, p. 172.

should not think our day-to-day decisions inconsequential, she seems to say, nor should we treat them as sombrely portentous.

Game playing is mentioned by Mrs Cadwallader in Chapter 37, where she comments on Mr Brooke and Will Ladislaw's establishment of the 'Pioneer' newspaper. 'It is frightful – this taking to buying whistles and blowing them in everybody's hearing', she tells Sir James Chettam, 'Lying in bed all day and playing at dominoes, like poor Lord Plessy, would be more private and bearable'.[16] Playing dominoes at least has the virtue of being unobtrusive, unlike the more public game-playing of Mr Brooke's contest against the established 'Trumpet' newspaper.

Casaubon (who is not, we suspect, entirely neutral in the matter) agrees in seeing journalism as disreputable. It compromises 'certain social fitnesses and proprieties', he declares, and therefore he will no longer accept Will at his house.[17]

This newspaper episode both celebrates and mocks the investment made by the novel's characters in the everyday life of Middlemarch and its surroundings. By making Will Ladislaw, who is modelled on the Romantic heroes of Byronic and German literature, a newspaperman, Eliot acknowledges a new importance for this most disposable, ephemeral sort of writing. But at the same time there is something slightly ridiculous in this descent of a potential Manfred or Childe Harold to the mundanity of writing about events in one small corner of England.

---

[16] *Middlemarch*, p. 315.
[17] *Middlemarch*, p. 309.

Mrs Cadwallader sums up her misgivings about the whole business when she tells Sir James, 'I said to Sir Humphrey long ago, Mr Brooke is going to make a splash in the mud. And now he has done it.'[18] In this metaphor of the blundering gentleman falling in the mud we have one of the most stereotyped of stock comic images, but also one that raises the question: who will get splashed?

The noble intentions of Will are here combined with the slapstick reality of Mr Brooke; the ripple of Icarus dropping into the water becomes the splat of a generously-proportioned behind falling into the mud. Eliot is aware that ordinary life is funny, and should be laughed at, but that does not mean it is without consequences.

The title of the novel also plays with ideas of the central and the marginal. With the word *middle*, *Middlemarch* seems to be telling us that it is interested in the most centrally important of events. And if that middle is *marching*, this is surely a book stridently addressing the pressing issues of the day. The word middle must also, given the Reform Act context of the narrative, make us think of the middle-class's increasing domination of English society, so that the novel is pointing towards a deeply meaningful shift in national history.

On the other hand, the title can be taken geographically, since the novel is set in the middle of the country – in and around Warwickshire. Warwickshire, though, is hardly central to the great proceedings of business and government that shape the nation. The midlands are more likely to be seen as backwards, as left behind, and so the title becomes

---

[18] *Middlemarch*, p. 315.

ironic or even comic (the middle marches on, but doesn't realise London is already out of sight).

Yet, on the third hand, if we start to think of margins rather than centres, the word *march* becomes important in a different way. 'Marches' refers to a border territory, such as the Welsh Marches for instance, so that the title is suggesting that the midlands are on the edge of something. Perhaps then, it is activating a tension between the 'middle' and the 'march', meaning edge. In this case we cannot tell whether we are speaking about something vitally important or something completely trivial.

This is a game I am playing with words, of course, but it has a point, since the novel is poised on just this border between importance and triviality. The title hints at what the lives of characters played out across the monumental sweep of *Middlemarch* will confirm: the everyday is worthy of our attention, yet at the same time world-historical events might be closer than we think. Equally importantly, this is a novel which reminds us that we might not always be able to tell the one from the other, and so to take neither one too seriously.

About the Contributor

Ben Moore is Assistant Professor of English Literature at the University of Amsterdam, where he teaches a range of BA and MA courses, including 'George Eliot and the Realist Novel'. He has published widely on Victorian literature, including in the journals *Victorian Literature and Culture*, *MLR*, *The Gaskell Journal* and *Dickens Quarterly*. He is working on a monograph entitled *Invisible Architecture*, which deals with cities and architecture in nineteenth-century literature

Valedictory

And We're Still Crazy about George Eliot

Paul Davies

This book has been a real labour of love – and we hope a fitting 200th birthday present for George Eliot – and her many readers and, we hope, her new readers.

The enthusiasm and pleasure, the challenge and the fulfilment that all of the authors of this book have displayed is genuine – and it has been a real pleasure to work with every one of the contributors to fashion this book out of a simple idea.

My thanks to everyone who has contributed – and wouldn't it be wonderful if we received emails from people who have really decided to pick up a George Eliot novel as a result of reading these words?

Do email – and I will ensure every author sees a copy of any that are sent.

And enjoy!

paul@bite-sizedbooks.com

Bite-Sized Lifestyle Books

Bite-Sized Lifestyle Books are designed to provide insights and ideas about our lives and the pressures on all of us and what we can do to change our environment and ourselves – and to celebrate life and success.

They are deliberately short and easy to read, helping readers gain a different perspective or develop new interests and experiences. They are firmly based on personal knowledge and where relevant successful actions.

Whether it is about a new skill or introducing new ideas into people's lives – the aim is to make them the *antidote to* **unread** *books* by making them easy to read, challenging and thought provoking – and usually optimistic.

They can be read straight through at one easy sitting or read and pondered over – but most of all they are written for enjoyment.

Bite-Sized Books Catalogue

Business Books

Lifestyle Books

Public Affairs Books

John Mair, Richard Keeble and Farrukh Dhondy (Editors)
V.S Naipaul:
The legacy
John Mills
Economic Growth Post Brexit
How the UK Should Take on the World
Christian Wolmar
Wolmar for London
Creating a Grassroots Campaign in a Digital Age

Fiction

Paul Davies
The Ways We Live Now
Civil Service Corruption, Wilful Blindness, Commercial
Fraud, and Personal Greed – a Novel of Our Times
Paul Davies
Coming To
A Novel of Self-Realisation
Victor Hill
Three Short Stories
Messages, The Gospel of Vic the Fish, The Theatre of
Ghosts

Children's Books

Chris Reeve – illustrations by Mike Tingle
The Dictionary Boy
A Salutary Tale
Fredrik Payedar
The Spirit of Chaos
It Begins

Made in the USA
Middletown, DE
18 December 2019